LIFE WITHOUT A RECIPE

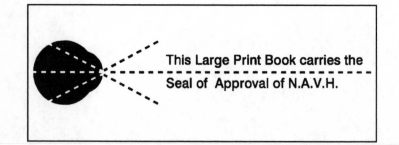

This Large Print Book carries the
Seal of Approval of N.A.V.H.

LIFE WITHOUT A RECIPE

A MEMOIR

DIANA ABU-JABER

THORNDIKE PRESS
A part of Gale, Cengage Learning

GALE
CENGAGE Learning®

Farmington Hills, Mich • San Francisco • New York • Waterville, Maine
Meriden, Conn • Mason, Ohio • Chicago

GALE
CENGAGE Learning®

LIBRARY OF CONGRESS CATALOGING-IN-PUBLICATION DATA

Names: Abu-Jaber, Diana.
Title: Life without a recipe : a memoir / by Diana Abu-Jaber.
Description: Large print edition. | Waterville, Maine : Thorndike Press, 2016. |
  Series: Thorndike Press large print biographies and memoirs
Identifiers: LCCN 2016003215 | ISBN 9781410489326 (hardcover) | ISBN 1410489329
  (hardcover)
Subjects: LCSH: Abu-Jaber, Diana. | Women authors, American—Biography. | Arab
  American women—Biography. | Large type books
Classification: LCC PS3551.B895 Z46 2016 | DDC 813/.54—dc23
LC record available at http://lccn.loc.gov/2016003215

Published in 2016 by arrangement with W. W. Norton & Company Ltd.

Published in the United States of America
1 2 3 4 5 6 7 20 19 18 17 16

To my daughter Gracie,
my star light,
and
To the memory of my grandmother,
Grace,
who lit my path

INTRODUCTION

The air was shaking. That's what it felt like
— enormous, roaring machinery, prowling
over the street. And just me, six years old,
limp-armed, stumped, mid-sidewalk. Usually there was a cloud of other first-graders
to walk home with, drifty and school-spent.
But today, alone, watching the machines
rear up, I backed away in horror and turned
down another street. It wasn't the way to
our house: I only knew one way — three
blocks straight, turn right, three blocks
straight. Nobody ever mentioned that one
day the turn-right might be filled with machines.

My thought was *Not that way.* So I walked
farther and farther from home. Until someone's mother looked out their window and
noticed me drooping along. She took me in
and called my parents on a kitchen phone
like ours with a curling cord attached to the
wall. Like a miracle, they appeared in the

drive, asking, "Where were you going?"

Perhaps there are other children who would have done the same thing — let their anxiety stop them in their tracks, turn them in exactly the wrong direction. Perhaps other children found the world as inscrutable as I did. As I grew up, clouds closed in — hours of running down the stairs trying to fly, of wishing for magical powers, of hunting for four-leafed clovers, not hearing the school bell, raising my head in the middle of the afternoon to find myself alone in a green field. The dreaminess, I think, was a cloak against fear, the sense of being unequal to the situation at hand.

Some kids are flattened by depression, others get angry; for me, there was a static-filled field of uncertainty. Then what do you do? What happens when, thanks to temperament or circumstances, the fit never feels right, and you're not at home in yourself? Underneath that is another question: Where is the other path?

The good neighbor sat me at a round Formica table, much like the one at home, and opened the fridge with its big, reassuring suck. Among a circle of other crazy-haired kids, I received my first sacrament of peanut butter and Fluffernutter sandwich — a craving instilled for years to come. I felt better at the table, which I thought of not just as a place to eat but also as a story-telling, argument-having place, useful and plain-faced and reassuring.

If the world is the water, the table is a raft; place your hands on it and hold on.

■ ■ ■ ■

PART I
GRACE AT THE TABLE

■ ■ ■ ■

CHAPTER ONE:
CRACK

Her small hand curves like eggshell: satin skin, round fingers, dimples in place of knuckles. The brown egg echoes her holding hand. My breath is there too, inside the curve of her holding, waiting for the crack.

"Why don't you let me, honey?"

"I can do it."

"Eggs are tricky."

"I can do it! Me! I can!"

I watch the small hand hover with treasure. The treasure isn't so much the egg, it's the cracking. It's using the sharp knife, prizing cookies off the hot tray, flipping the pancake. If it's difficult and risky, it's delicious.

"All right. But remember how I showed you?"

The hand lifts, hesitates, then smashes the egg nearly flat against the cutting board. Crushed egg and shell everywhere. For a moment, she's paralyzed. Then her eyes turn to mine, her mouth opens into a squared-off silent wail. Finally the sob. Friends marveled at how passionately she cried as a newborn, weeping true tears weeks before babies are supposed to be able to produce them. After the shock wears off and we clean the counters (she helps, making smooth, even lines with a sponge), she is ardent to try again.

This time my hand rides hers, rising together. Now the crack is more temperate. Mostly egg spills into the bowl, long strings of it hanging from fingers. She wipes them neatly on my pants leg. We stare at the yolk in the bowl. "Hey, you did it!"

"What is that? Down there?" Hovering on her step stool, she cranes her neck.

There's only egg in the bowl. "What do you mean? Just eggs." But maybe I understand: Something about cracking it yourself makes you see it differently. There's a little bit of sadness in it. She asks these sorts of obscurantist questions that are like fishing, in which neither of us quite understands what she's after. But I try to answer anyway.

"What does it make?"

"You mean what does egg . . . become? Turn into? Everything. Everything comes out of an egg."

"What does?"

"Animals. Chickens. Snakes. Fish. People do. You started with an egg. Just a really teensy one."

"No I didn't," she says. She sounds distracted. Tilting the big ceramic bowl, she might be considering the beginning of life, the ends of the cosmos. The whorl at the center of the batter. A bowl is a place to find meaning, I think. Stir the spoon and wait, all sorts of things rise to the mind's surface. I used to joke that I wanted a child so I'd have someone to bake with. Perhaps not such a big joke. The first time my grandmother handed me an egg to crack, I was five. I thanked her, admired it, then tried to hand it back, wary of that hard white thing.

My daughter asks for a fork so she can pop the eyeball.

I hand it over and she stabs the yolk: stab, stab, stab.

Every year between Halloween and Christmas, my grandmother Grace transforms her apartment into a bakery. Tables and chairs are covered with racks of cooling cookies, eight baking sheets slip in and out of the oven — as tiny as something in a troll's house. The Mixmaster drones. A universe of cookies: chocolate-planted peanut butter;

15

sinus-kicking bourbon balls; reindeer and sugar bells; German press-form cookies from her grandparents' Bavarian village — *Springerle* — green wreaths, candy berries; and a challenging, grown-uppy variety named for the uncut dough's sausage shape: *Wurstcakes*. All part of Grace's arsenal: she's engaged in an internecine war with my father, Bud, over the loyalties of the children. Her Wurstcakes are slim as communion wafers. Bud dunks them in his demitasse of *ahweh* and calls them "Catholic cookies." Her eyes tighten as she watches him eat.

"Only higher civilizations bake cookies," she says to me, raking fingers through the shrubbery of my hair. "I don't know how you people would celebrate Christmas if I wasn't around. Run wild like savages."

My parents were married in Gram's church. When the priest presented Dad with a contract to raise his children within the Catholic faith, Dad signed in Arabic. He nudged Gram in the ribs, as if she were in on the joke, and, instead of his name, wrote: *I make no promises.* In my parents' satiny wedding photographs, Grace stared at Bud. *I'm on to you, friend.*

"Never learn how to sew, cook, type, or iron." She bends over the board, passes the

16

hissing iron back and forth, slave rowing a galley ship. "That's how they get you." She pauses long enough to turn that shrewd gaze on me and after a moment I look away. There's cooking, sure, but then there's baking. I learn from Grace that sugar represents a special kind of freedom. It charms almost everyone; it brings love and luck and good favor. Cakes and cookies are exalted — a gift of both labor and sweetness — so good a smart woman is willing to give herself to them.

Adversaries, even enemies, can rely on each other. My father and my grandmother teach me this by accident. They don't get along and they agree on everything. Especially the two essentials:

1. Men are terrible.
2. Save your money (Gram: in bra. Bud: somewhere, preferably not at the horse races).

Also, they both want all the love. As if there is a limited supply and never enough to go around. They wrangle over the children's souls and both set out food for us, bait inside a trap. Bud cooks — earthy, meaty dishes with lemon and oil and onion. Gram is more ruthless — she pries open those foil-lined tins, cookies covered with sugar crystals like crushed rubies, the beckoning finger of vanilla. I think about the story of the witch in her gingerbread house, how she schemed to push Hansel and Gretel into her oven. Gram reads me the story; I sit, rapt, watching her, her sky-blue eyes glittering. *I will fight anyone for you,* she seems to say. Even if it means cooking you and gobbling you up.

Bud doesn't quite grasp the concept of this fight; his wrath is more episodic. Anything that strikes him as American-disrespectful — say, one of us kids gives him the old eye-roll, or an "oh, yuh" — and he'll be shouting the cupboards off the walls. Then he'll storm into the kitchen and fill it with the scent of cauliflower seething in olive oil and garlic, the bitter, sulfurous ingredients he hacks up when he's in a mood. Stuff that tastes like punishment to an eight-year-old. Most of the time, though, when Grace is around he forgets there's a war on. He argues casually, conversationally, segues into off-handed, cheerful observations and questions: "Why do cookies always come in circles?" Etc. This deepens her rage and despair — he can't even be bothered to remember that they're fighting.

So disrespectful!

Grace is vigilant, tallying all those casual betrayals between men and women, as if she were jotting them in a notebook. It's not just Bud, it's all of them. Men as a general category are disappointing and traitorous — in money and family and work and power. Romantic love is another of their snares. "They tell you to wait, wait, wait," she says. "True love will come. True love will make everything so much better. So you wait and wait and wait, and true love turns out to be a nincompoop with a venereal disease."

The insults, the sharp little arrows seem to be everywhere, even in places and moments that seem the most innocent. Gram will take me to see Snow White of the limpid flesh and cretinous voice — and the Prince with the powerful shoulders who must save her from another woman — an old lady! — and raise the helpless thing, literally, from the dead. Gram mutters, "Flibbertigibbet." Afterward, we go to a café where they bring us crepes with cherries and whipped cream. "Did you see," she grouses. "Those dwarves, they only wanted her to stay *after* she offered to cook for them."

Only a few of us in the family understand

how those crisply divided feelings, love and complaint, float together, united. All grudges are softened by the approach of dinner. Those who labor with Bud in the kitchen are joined in a confederacy — cooking restores us to our senses. During the week, my father works two or more jobs. But Saturday breakfast is a profusion: the sizzling morsels of lamb on the fava beans; diced tomato, celery, and onion on the hummus; tidy, half-fried eggs bundled around their yolks. We hurry to sit and then spend half the meal begging Bud, "Come to the table! Sit down. *Sit.*" Always, he wants to slice one more cucumber.

Throughout my childhood, I hear Americans joke about Bud and his harem — his wife and three daughters. He laughs, strong white teeth; he says, "Don't forget my mother-in-law."

Before they'd met, neither Grace nor Bud could have imagined each other, not once in a million years. They came with their ingredients like particles of lost and opposing worlds, the dying old divisions — East and West.

Among my father's library of made-up true stories is a favorite, about meeting his mother-in-law:

Grace was not pleased about her only

child falling in with this questionable young man with a mustache. But that was a separate issue from good manners and laying out a nice table for company. At the time, the fanciest dish Grace knew of was shrimp poached in a wine and butter sauce. My father, most recently of the semiarid village of Yahdoudeh, studied the pale, curling bodies on the plate and saw a combination of cockroach and scorpion; he also deduced that the older lady with the stiff blonde hair and see-through eyes was some sort of *bruja*. He ate only the sweet dinner rolls — which were quite good — and left the rest untouched. Bud somehow had himself a marvelous time, even with the *bruja*'s blue eye fixed on him. Maybe because of it. Afterward, mortally offended, Grace scraped shrimp into the garbage, her throat filled with a dark will for revenge.

A few months later, my poor mother, Patty, barely twenty years old, eternal optimist, proposed a do-over: this time in honor of their engagement. Grace decided to pull out all the stops. Telling her version, my grandmother had said, "You know how that is — the more you hate someone the nicer you are to them?" To her, there was nothing better than a glistening, pink ham. In anguish, she slathered it with brown

21

sugar and pineapple slices, voodoo-piercing it with cloves — each a tiny dart.

My Muslim father stood at the table, staring at the ham — forbidden, "unclean" meat. As soon as Gram saw his expression, she went to the phone book and jotted down the address of the White Castle. She swore she'd had no idea of this dietary restriction. "Who doesn't eat *ham*?" she'd cried twenty years later, still in disbelief. "I was so angry, I was almost laughing."

Bud brought back fries for the table.

You want most what you can't have. Gram would fight him for her daughter, long after the fight was over.

When I am nine, I cook a leg of lamb for my grandmother. A whole leg, just the two of us, but it's important because, in my mind, it's a possible culinary meeting place for him and her. When I suggest it, Gram says *Oh!* She *adores* leg of lamb. She hasn't had it in for*ever*. This is the first dinner I've ever cooked for her. All day I fan away her questions and suggestions. I'm as bossy and kitchen-difficult as my dad. For hours, the big joint burbles in wine and vinegar on top of the stove and fills her apartment with a round, heady scent that makes you weak-kneed. I set the table carefully, with napkins

22

and water glasses. I carve and plate the lamb on top of the stove, then carry it out and place it before her.

She lowers her fork after a few bites, her mouth wilting.

"What's wrong?" I'd crushed each garlic clove — a whole head — with salt, pepper, snips of rosemary, and had slipped the paste into slits in the meat, just the way I'd seen my father do. The tender meat breaks into fragments beneath the fork; I could drink the braising sauce with a spoon. "What did I do?"

Gram takes off her glasses and knuckles the corners of her eyes. Finally she says, "I like my lamb *rare*. With mint *jelly*." Her voice is pure pout. She sounds like my four-year-old sister, parked on the top step shouting, "Nobody loves me! You're not the boss of me!" Rummaging through accusations until she finds whatever lines up with the way she feels inside, abandoned in the hard world.

At nine, it's only just beginning to occur to me that I'm on my own here. The adults give you what they can, richer or poorer. Mint jelly! It is accusation and insult. She has detected my father's hand in the sauce. Affronted, I want to slap the table, bluster away, just like my dad does. But how do you argue with mint jelly? I took a risk and failed. It had never occurred to me that tastes and preferences could be so embedded in personality and history.

To me, deliciousness is still a simple matter — I don't have enough experience yet to understand how personal such things are. How you must choose the ingredients and tools slowly, putting together a palate, just as you build a life. Taste is desire, permitted or not, encouraged or not. There is no arguing it away, there is no winner in this fight, no recipe to follow. There is only blind faith and improvisation.

CHAPTER TWO:
WORK

My grandmother has no ambivalence, no division: you answer the call of work, whether it's the sort you are called to or the sort you have to do. She's disdainful of housekeeping, yet her lavender-colored apartment glows, wiped down with lemon water. Hand-crank windows; a magical TV secreted inside an oak cabinet; fat, unbudgeable pieces of furniture; everything Pledged. And then the evidence of other work: her closets aromatic with talcs and colognes and sachets and new pajamas — gifts from the parents of her students. Neatly stacked and unopened. Years of grade-school teaching filed in pajama sets.

The true work, the work she's called to, is in the infernally hot kitchen.

Grace understood herself better when she baked. She settled into herself and heard her inner voice more clearly. Baking can become a bigger conversation, in which the mind rambles far and wide; you consider not only the amount of sugar but the way it glitters, the smell of its dust as you level it with the cup. Grace spoke of the elegant process of following a recipe, step by step, to some satisfying conclusion. Of course, that wasn't my style: I couldn't leave a recipe in peace, but had to be continually worrying it and playing with it.

When I'm six, she turns to study me over a recipe card. I don't want to use chocolate chips in the batter, I want to mince a big, black chocolate bar the way I saw our Italian neighbor do it. And then I want to chop cherries and scrape those in as well. After a moment of internal struggle, Gram says, "You're a composer-type, dahlin." I get this is not such a great thing. She examines the stained recipe card for pudding cake and admits in a light voice, "I prefer to play it safe. I'm just a journeyman."

In my grandmother's world, journeyman is a humble yet not undesirable role. A journeyman is stout and honest and brave: a hard worker. There is the fork in Grace's road, between romance and work. Romance is beguiling, a beautiful, wicked witch. Work can be exaltation or drudgery, but it's always finer, smarter, more soul-satisfying than the lie that is romance.

■ ■ ■ ■

I haven't found out yet that people can fashion multiple lives, pile them up like china in a cabinet. Surely, Gram has always been here with her lovely tiny oven, tiny juice pitcher, and her bitty disappointing fridge, crammed with plastic-wrapped crumbs — in which we girls are not allowed to rummage or disport, for fear of disrupting her "system."

Surely she has always been *Gram.* (And how startling, when I hear her tell someone that she now has to "get used to" saying she's sixty. Hasn't she always known she was old?) Every now and then I hear someone call her Grace, and it's like catching a glimpse of some hidden origin, another long-ago self. She tells and tells me about this other life, a fairy tale that took place in the time of the Garden State — when that moniker wasn't a punch line. The places my grandmother talks about — Elizabeth, Roselle, Linden — sound pleasing and feminine. There was a porch on the house. Purple blossoms rolled across the painted floor. Maple seeds whirled, horse chestnuts, and fine, full Dutch elms lined the block like hopeful ladies at a dance, and no one could imagine that one day they would gather their limbs and wither away.

The way she tells it, her life's one big romance was ruined by deception. But then I think she would see it that way because anger is such a big part of her: I don't know who my grandmother would be without her anger.

"He saw me going into the bank building downtown. I always wore a nice dress and a good coat, so he thought I was rich." Gram sucks at the insides of her cheeks, her face long and droll. We're working on an angel food, my favorite among favorites for its texture. A wish of a cake, which vanishes on the tongue. Lifting the pan, gently turning it in midair, she shows me how to invert it. I know the pads of her fingers are burning through the useless, hemstitched potholders.

"He watched me go in and out that building." She has a private way of telling some stories, as if she's talking to herself. I stare: It's hard to fathom a time Gram might've wanted much besides cake and ice cream, and, possibly, bowling. "So *chaarming*. Ach. Those blue eyes. Like the ocean! Like the devil's, says my sister Alyce. He was the charming, drunken, Irish milkman. Back then I didn't know — to be careful, I mean.

I didn't know the first thing. Ach, the charming ones." She shakes her head at me; I feel it, an ache in the chest.

He thought she was going to the bank, and in all that time she was going to the second floor, the office above the bank, to see her dentist. Getting her teeth drilled and pulled, until the not-too-distant day when she would have to glue dentures to her gums. But back then she still had teeth. "And a lovely shape. Always size six." In the wedding photograph, the sepia tone makes the serious young people look evanescent, their skin too pale, their eyes transparent. Beside her brothers and sisters in their stylish suits, my grandmother's expression is transported, unconfined, lifted slightly to the left. Beside her, my grandfather looks directly at the camera. Smirks.

After just a few years of marriage, my grandmother developed a stitch in her joints, arcs of pain wracked one knee. She couldn't stand. In the hospital, they discovered she had an "infection." She brings her face close to mine as we sit at the table, waiting for our cake to cool and firm, trapping air that will keep it aloft after we turn it over. "It was a *venereal disease,*" she breathes, her gaze scorching. And there's more. "While I was in the hospital — full of penicillin — *he* clears out our bank accounts. He goes to the house and snatches my jewelry. Leaves me high and dry. Heads out with Deirdre Miller, who's the mother of one of my own students. Married woman, no less." She sniffs. "He'd been sleeping with this one and that. All over town. He gave it to me and then toodleloo." Left destitute, she and her little girl moved back in with her parents. My mother grew up in that shared bedroom while my grandmother rebuilt herself, enduring lashes of emotion hot as anything the nuns described waiting in hell. The neighbors' hushed voices; pitying smiles from the other teachers; her father's stark face, his black German mustache. Penitent, exile, prisoner, she ate and drank the memory of betrayal — the man had poisoned her hopes for love, cast a pall over her younger unmarried sisters, sullied the family name. "I should've known. But how could I know?" She echoes the long-ago voices that ringed the old house, their judgment, her feeble self-defense. She says, voice fragile, "Maybe if I was more special? Prettier? Or maybe even smarter. . . ."

I sense, deep in my ten-year-old self, what she is trying to say, and I fling my arms around her middle, squeeze the air out so her laughter is half-gasp. "Grammy! You're

30

perfect!"

So even my grandmother tumbled down into the thorns, the sharp heart of desire, let herself be snagged by hope and mad promises of romance. For all her anger and abiding suspicion, there was a time when even she had gotten caught up. It shouldn't be a surprise, I suppose, that the angriest people are the ones with the highest, most bitterly dashed hopes — like fairy-tale kings who banish music from kingdoms after the beloved dies. But Grace saved herself and my mother. She did. She held her head up, and she reported to work, and she made sure her girl's hair was combed and her face washed. And oh, if she twirled sugar, butter, and salt together, just so, therein was found ease and pleasure and another kind of love — the kind that you make for yourself, the kind that delivers on promises and asks almost nothing in return. This was how work saved her — the true work, the kind that takes you so deeply and happily into yourself, away from all the other troubles and unsolvable sorts of hurt, and keeps you sound.

We loosen the cake from the pan edges, flip it onto a cake plate. Grace wants to drizzle chocolate glaze, the way, she says, Irma Rombauer — author of her exalted

Joy of Cooking — would do it. But I want a dusting of confectioners' sugar. "It looks like a blizzard," I say, shaking the sifter so sugar goes in a puff everywhere. Her mouth twists but she lets me have my way. She says I'm "creative." That comes first. We cut the cake with the serrated knife; she takes the piece from the side that isn't quite as high as the rest — as she will, eating our burnt toast, the stringy or undercooked or unripe bites. Because even though she is angry and full of will and power, we are her prize, the granddaughters.

"The worst thing you can do to your life. . . ." Gram closes her eyes, inhales cake as you might a bouquet. "The worst thing? Is to get married."

I'm ten and this isn't what I want to hear. "But — what if you're *in love*?"

"Love is different." Then she scowls. "What? Are you planning to be in love now?"

"Well, not this second, I mean. But what about babies and stuff?"

She shrugs before adding chocolate sprinkles to the sugar. "Babies are fine. Babies are for women who can't do much else."

Not far away, there is another kitchen for me, another kind of work to do. The smells

32

of cooking remind me I should be chopping, clearing, setting the table, not hiding in my bedroom, hunched over the bed with a notebook. There are houseguests, my father's relatives, arguing politics in the living room, a fragrance of rice and zataar, chopped onions, pine nuts fried in butter floating over their heads. So much argument and advice! In this place, children and adults reside on separate planets, only occasionally crossing paths in the kitchen, just close enough for someone to lean down, lifting an instructional finger:

"Work hard, save your money," my father says. Though I've never known him to follow the second part of that advice.

"Drink the best wine first," Uncle Jack offers, "while you still can taste it."

"Say yes to the Americans, always oh yes sir. But when they turn around — poof!" Uncle Hal lifts his foot. "Boot 'em in the behind."

"Don't have kids." That's my Aunt Rachel, an English professor and much-esteemed mother of favorite cousins Jess and Ed. "They wreck everything." She says it so matter-of-factly, but there's a joke inside everything she says. Like the Bugs Bunny cartoons — two jokes, the one on top for children, the hidden one for grown-ups. "Children are a luxury women can't afford." Aunt Rachel read the novel I wrote in fourth grade and says there's hope for me yet.

"But men can?"

She looked at me from the corners of her long, Russian eyes. "That's why they have wives."

In the land of *Min Eedi,* children are coddled and bullied, doted upon and dominated. *Min eedi* means "from my hand": my uncles eat Bedouin-style, standing around the platter of mensaf. Their wives — some American, like Aunt Rachel, some Jordanian — teach and write and work and work. Uncle Hal scoops a bit of lamb, some rice and onion, and tosses it lightly in the palm of his right hand. He brings the impromptu dumpling to his fingertips, turns to one of the children, and says, "Here. *Min eedi.*" We open our mouths to be fed these occasional bites, too hot and too much food at once, and you can't refuse such a special honor, but at the same time you also don't really want it.

Soaking in advice, awash in it. I become infected with second-guessing; instinct floats like a thread on the surface of the eye; all decisions are fraught. I'm told to be brave and free, to write fearlessly, live independently. But then again, be careful, careful, careful. Advice is offered like food from the hand — a loving, unwanted gift.

The more my grandmother warns about men, the more I huff and sigh, mutter *man-hater* under my breath. The more someone warns you not to do something, the more you want to do it — luscious as a poisoned apple — it wants biting.

Bud, on the other hand, doesn't trifle with warnings. He forbids tomfoolery, dalliance, and boys. Any invitation to a party, dance, sleepover is flapped in the air.

"You don't know what they're capable of." Bud, foreboding.

"Who?" I can't help asking, though I know the answer well.

"Boys!"

"But *you're* a guy, Dad."

"That's how I know!"

Bud's bad-craziness is also his good-craziness. He stares at his wife and daughters as if he can't believe this great fortune. The idea of letting America tamper with us, lure his children away, the idea of us growing up into Americans, is a little unbearable. So he's vigilant. A guardian and protector, he's had to learn how to live by his wits and he wants to show us his tricks.

Perhaps it's because he was one of the youngest among a rowdy gang of brothers. He tells me and my sisters, "My mother brought a pot of chicken to the front of the table and those boys went crazy. They used to say, 'Watch your fingers!' " When it got down to the littlest boys, the pot would be reduced to scraps. They fought over the fatty tail, they cracked open the bones and sucked out the marrow. He shows us these hiding places, the last succulent bites — "oysters" of meat secreted in the chicken back. He gestures for us to lean in over the dinner table and, with a cagey smile, he murmurs, "Nobody knows. Don't forget — those are the best parts."

I lean against the swath of his back as he combs the bulgur wheat. If you try to cook in his kitchen, he stares over your shoulders, but he'll let you help clean. Maybe chop an onion. "You have to search the bulgur so carefully," he says, pointing here and there. The tiniest, hardest stones hide inside the grains. Bits of sand that look just like bulgur. "That's how life is!" he says with a swoop of his hand, mysterious. Usually answering some other thing that no one asked.

I sit with him, helping him comb. When you cover the grains with water, a kind of starchy mist swirls around your fingers: I see goats with fishtails, all sorts of creatures from my relatives' stories. Oryx, unicorns, fairies. Which are real and which aren't? The metamorphosis of cooking mirrors that of story-imagining. I learn to watch carefully for the stones, and sometimes stories come to me, emerging out of the starch, and explain things.

Instead of going to dances and parties, I stay home and write. By the time I'm in high school, I've written pages and pages and pages. Boxloads. In my junior year, I discover that somehow I have enough school credits to escape.

Sixteen years old, I enroll at the state university up the road. This is where my Jordanian uncles like to send their kids for American-college. Uncle Hal teaches here, so they think it's safe. I have immigrant cousins everywhere, nearly one in each class: *Magnum P.I.* mustaches; eyes lively, black, and narrow as whips; everyone restless. Boys tote plastic cups foggy with beer. The lovely smell of old, sour beer is all over the place. I like being in places I'm not supposed to be. The first time a boy tries to kiss me with an open mouth, I jerk back, guffawing like he'd hit me with a joy buzzer.

When I see the look on his face, I take a breath and say, "Okay. Do over."

In my sophomore year, the writer John Gardner comes to speak at the college. At a reception in a faculty house, I ambush him with a stack of typewritten pages. I ask, voice wobbling, if he'd maybe, someday, glance at my story. To my disbelief, he groans and patiently lowers himself into a chair at the kitchen table. For long minutes he sits there, hunched in a leather jacket, shoulder-length white hair falling forward, his soft, thought-creased face tipped over the pages. He stops me later, story in hand. "I wrote down a few things for you here." A sheet filled with handwritten notes. Eventually the notes go astray, but his advice remains: Graduate studies. Daily writing. Hone the craft.

Also, this at the end of the comments, written in soft pencil: You better choose — because you're a woman — between writing and having a family.

Gardner's injunctions play in my head, a spare, repeating melody. I accept his directives without question. I'm not overly concerned; I believe I've already made my choice. Writing is essential as a nutrient. And at nineteen, the idea of children is a distant planet.

■ ■ ■ ■

Senior year, Jeremy and I share a house because it cuts the rent in half. I have no real romantic interest in him, but no way to grasp or measure this. Our rare couplings are quick and confusing to both of us: I confess to sometimes trying to read through it all, holding a book open over Jeremy's head. Aside from a few select cousins, I've never been allowed to have friends who were boys; at this point, men are a novelty, an offbeat pleasure. Jeremy is sort of a poet. He writes odd, elliptical little paragraphs, which my professor-uncle Hal once observed didn't "add up to much." Also, he sometimes sports a turban with a rhinestone in the center. He used to have waist-length, red hair, but at a recent party, Jeremy sat on the lawn with a pair of scissors and chopped off his hair in three swoops, then fed it to the fire like a human sacrifice.

In our yearlong sorta relationship, Jeremy and I have discussed the whole-wheat-bread recipe in the *Moosewood Cookbook,* whether to put peas in the carbonara, and the steaming techniques in our latest discovery, a blue tome called *The International Cookbook.* Our cooking lab is an exploration of the creative process. Gradually, I'm seeing how the process can be nudged into a discipline.

On an early spring day during senior year, we prepared a watered-down version of Peking duck and steamed pork buns. Even modified, the meal is too expensive and difficult for us, but we've been cooking together for nearly a year and have learned a little bit about how to make meals seem greater than the sum of their parts. Jack, Moss, and Isaac have arrived on their Harleys, noise churning the air. Jeremy is twenty-two; his friends are impressively older — from twenty-seven to thirty. Fully grown adults, they showed up in 1980, after the war in Vietnam, each making his way to the university, funded by the GI Bill. We sit on the floor around our table — a steamer trunk — trying to roll up the duck in pancake. Foreignness, we hope, makes things more delicious. Jack hears a sound out front and lifts his hands so all the men look at him and stop talking. The stillness in their eyes is instant and far reaching: It's something I've noticed on previous occasions, as if there's a sliver in each of them that is terribly old, as if that one piece has absorbed the sadness in their bodies. When it surfaces, I feel within myself a corresponding swirl, a drop of ink in a glass of water.

We freeze, listening, and the sound comes again: *Diana!*

I go to the door: Uncle Hal stands about ten feet back in the middle of the front lawn. A big, healthy man in his early sixties, he straddles a battered Schwinn with a bell and streamers attached to the handlebars. Look closely, you'll find a homemade price tag stuck to one of the fenders. He pulls a small box out of his pocket. "O niecie, I got you something."

He wants to have a conference on the lawn, but the men emerge, shouting, "Professor Abu!" Shaking his hand. There are several reasons why Uncle Hal avoids entering my house. It's shabby and musty, and seeing the inside will indict my housekeeping, but, more important, it will reveal evidence of a man. When Bud and Hal refer to themselves as Bedouins, it means, among other things, that they adhere to a grizzled old moral code: Their daughters are to remain virginal up to the last breath before they're married off. Easier to use the Jordanian telegraph system — yelling from the yard — than risk uncovering something you already knew.

They tow Uncle Hal into the living room.

The vets love Uncle, his loud, profane, angry lectures on world politics pinning students to their seats, his roaring indignation at America — its greed, ignorance, corruption — and the suffering of developing countries at the hands of the so-called first world. Hal sits on the futon and looks quietly and unhappily over the proceedings. "What's all this bamboozling?"

"Peking duck." Jeremy offers him a plate, but my uncle merely tsks and huffs and drops his eyebrows: *You must be out of your mind.*

"I just came to give you this." The box in his fingertips. "I found it at a yard sale in Hannibal. It's real. All kinds of gold. I got the old lady down to $25! So we can . . . fix it — fix up this situation." His gaze floats to the ceiling. Both Uncle Hal and Bud know and don't know that I'm sharing a house with a man.

The box is dark indigo. I watch my hands move as though they belonged to someone else. The lid lifts, revealing a yellow-gold band. The breath rushes out of my chest: I stop moving. My uncle pulls the ring from the cardboard backing. I know he isn't completely sure which of the guys there is the boyfriend. In this velvet box, from somewhere deep in a widow's semiattached garage, he's found a good deal on gold, plus an answer to one of these confounding American problems. He urges me to try on the ring; naturally, it fits. "We can wrap tape around it if it's too big. Too small is more of a problem," he says. "This is a gift — from Uncle to you. Now it's all yours!"

The universe shrinks to the size of that tiny box, the box into which my life would fit. Uncle Hal is nodding and waving me off as I hold it out. He leans away — it's radioactive. After a moment of silence, Moss, Jack, and Fred start laughing, slapping each other on the back. Jeremy's mouth opens and closes fish-style — he looks at me, we're drowning in air.

After Uncle Hal's visit, we will spend a few days laughing about it. Then one afternoon, after we watch a sitcom in which the main characters attend a poodle wedding and end up accidentally and hilariously married to each other, Jeremy will turn to me, a dreamy, floaty half-smile on his face, and say, "But what if we just did it? Got all married?"

I will say, "Yeah perfect. Prearranged marriage." But the more we joke, the more Jeremy will seem to talk himself into it. "Really though, maybe we should? Imagine the party!" Bashful and nonchalant, he will say, "And it's almost the end of classes — are you gonna move back home?"

I see it before me, fully revealed: the end of college. Looking at the ring box, I experience a sort of vertigo, a sense of toppling into a chasm I'd never noticed opening at my feet. My grandmother had promised that work saves you — that a career lifts you out of circumstances, no matter how bad, that it gives you money, status, direction, community. Where exactly is that career? Now I grasp the folly of majoring in something like English literature. There's no internship, no entry-level opening under that heading. Throughout my childhood, Bud had insisted that I should go to law school or learn a "trade." But just a week ago, he'd pointed at a couple of little boys in a diner, faces smeared with ketchup like tribal marks. "Soon, I want you to get me some of those." It was as if he'd swept away all those other ambitions and revealed his true plan.

The thought of moving back home stops my breath, an image of black water closing over my head. The ring box is dark as a depthless pool — would this bring more freedom or less? Anything seems possible in these tipping moments. I don't know how much power I have, because a dutiful child, a girl child, doesn't have power. Perhaps my uncle was offering a way forward.

I called her to break the big news. Right away, she said to me, "I know what you're doing."

My chest tightened. "Oh, uh-hunh, it's so terrible," I said. "I'm marrying a great guy."

"You're trying to survive your father." Water was rushing in the background; her least favorite chore. She was washing dishes out of spite.

"Gram." I held the phone half an inch from my ear. "Can't this just be a good thing?"

Dishes clanked and rattled. "He doesn't still control you anymore. You don't have to let him push you around."

"I *want* to do this!" My voice sounded hot and loud in the phone.

All I could hear was splashing. It felt good to fill up with indignation — it crowded out other more complicated feelings. But then she relented. "It's fine. You're right. I just want you to be happy, dahlin."

"Thank you. I am happy."

"However you have to do it."

A dress like a spool of frosting. Two hundred people. The New Jersey relations. At the ceremony, in a church where we'd not once attended services, in a trance-state, Jeremy and I place the gold crowns on each other's heads, link pinkies, circle the altar, light candles, kiss. I can't look at him; his crown makes my eyes well with unintentional laughter. For the month of planning leading up to the wedding, this kept happening to me — unexpected, eye-watering hysterics at impossible moments. My mouth hurts from biting my lips. In the reception line, my grandmother crosses her arms and mutters, "This is the last time I will ever again wear a skirt."

I suspect Jeremy is in love, though not so much with me as with my distracting, contentious family: with my father's lamb-stuffed zucchini and my uncles' backyard philosophizing, and the parties in which pots become musical instruments and the boozy sessions of araq with the cousins, and tracing the stars with a finger, and the dreams of lost countries rising over the clothesline with the moon, which, my Aunt Aya swears, looks different in Jordan, like a golden goblet. Perhaps he thinks that when we marry he too will become a lyrical, disaffected Jordanian. A poet.

At the reception, the waiters bring out platters of stuffed cabbages studded with pomegranate seeds, grilled pigeon with tarragon, mensaf in yogurt sauce with toasted almonds, lemon-marinated shish kabobs, tiny crisp koftas, minced raw kibbeh, lamb chops redolent of garlic and chili. And chocolate wedding cake. After dinner, to our astonishment, the custodial staff steps forth brandishing long swords and performs a Bedouin dance, swishing and bowing, thrusting and parrying. Two hundred aunties kiss my cheeks, both sides several times, slap them lightly, smooth my hair, lift my eyelids, stare X-rays into my eyes, and tell me the babies will be tremendous. "Gigantic American babies!" Aunt Souhaf observes. The uncles and cousins slap Jeremy on the back, laughing and laughing and saying nothing. My grandmother strolls around the hall in a tasteful brocaded suit, glaring.

Most dishes aren't written down: They hover in the memory, a bit of contrail, the ends uncertain. What lingers are the traces, the way the vanilla dallied with the ginger, fading from the tongue like a last thread of salt. The taste, as it's remembered and passed down, can rarely be duplicated; the steps are mislaid, the ingredients tampered with. The taste is desire itself, the yearning for completion, in love or sugar or blood.

Each recipe is someone else's mistake or discovery. Angry and self-aware, bound to her oven, Grace knew what she needed. She was a journeyman and a proud one. She tried to tell me and I tried to listen. I did. All those hours of talking and scraping down the sides of the bowl were still inside of me. But no one wants to believe they'll make the same mistakes as others do. I thought I'd chosen the right course — already so certain I understood myself better than anyone ever could.

CHAPTER THREE:
DESIRE

"Let nothing but nothing stop you," my grandmother said. So many precarious elements to her life: an older woman, divorced and living alone, at a time when that wasn't much in favor. Sometimes she got unnerved — long-distance phone calls made her fretful about the expense, and she gave up completely on driving cars. Still, there was something unstoppable in her: After retirement, she trekked around the world on her own, took a prop plane to the high end of Alaska; crisscrossed Eastern Europe; sailed the Panama Canal. There was a "dalliance" with a performer on a cruise ship — to her grandchildren's amazement. They wrote to each other for years afterward, their letters purple with euphemism. In crucial ways, she seemed fearless.

One summer, Gram took me along to Paris, so I could "get culture." She'd never visited and had decided my indifferent language studies would suffice. Once we arrived, though, the trip turned into an investigation of boulangeries and patisseries. We glanced at the Louvre and the Eiffel Tower on our way to bake shops — tiny places with polished stone floors, wooden counters, and indelibly delicious cakes. There were fruit aspics and meringue twirled like whipped hairdos and mousses shaped like birds and starfish and Impressionist paintings in marzipan.

We went to the shops as early as she could roust me out of bed — usually by orange sunrise — and visited two, three, four bakeries in a day. We poked around corners, down alleyways, tottered over cobblestones, up the broad sidewalk of the Champs-Élysées, a guidebook and torn map fluttering in the breeze. Even through the oily city rain, we could smell the shops on approach, each with its particular scent of rising dough, baked fruit, roasting sugars. Gram leaned on the glass cases, looked toward the swinging doors to the oven, calling for the baker. If one emerged — blinking, uncertain, antisocial — she introduced herself. These men, glowering as if awakened from hibernation, claimed not to speak English. This didn't deter Grace from talking and talking to them.

Perhaps there was something compelling about my grandmother's refusal to believe in language barriers, or possibly some charm in her puffed blond hair, purple lipstick, cornflower-blue eyes, her jaunty lavender outfits, her kimono-style pajama suits. Maybe it was the novelty of being invited out front. In any case, eventually the bakers drifted nearer the counter, arms folded over barrel chests, chins tucked, and began to demand particulars.

"You are from where?" One man barked at us over a counter in the Latin Quarter. "Why are you here?"

I struggled to translate. I'd taken French for years but quickly learned I didn't know anything — the language, as spoken by actual native speakers, dissolved into a murk of vowels and gestures.

"Why are you dressed like that?" he asked my grandmother, gesturing at her head. "If you go uncovered, you'll get too much of the sun — it's unhealthy."

"Tell him," Gram dictated carefully, "we don't wear babushkas in America!"

The baker was dressed in an immaculate apron, his white jacket straining at the buttons. A flat-topped toque flopped forward on his brow. He bore a slight resemblance to Bud — many of the French did — round faces, olive skin, sleepy hooded eyes. When I mentioned this to Gram in the Latin Quarter shop, she said, "Please, don't ruin it."

"How old are you?" the baker asked Gram. "Where is your husband? How many children do you have?" He had such a frank, evaluative manner it seemed natural that he'd want to know these things — as if he were sizing up Gram like a basket of berries. Gram squinted at rows of apricot tarts nested in doilies as she offered her vital statistics. She used to tell me that priests were the best sorts of men, because they had "no appetites." Yet in our tour of bakeries, it seemed she was drawn to men who were nothing but appetite. When Parisians bowed before the oven, I felt they were doing something more than merely baking, something important and secret.

The baker went in back and returned with two slim loaves, which he buttered then spread with a jam black with fruit and sugar. On this, he layered a soft cheese and some sort of meat shaved to translucence, then squashed and cut the sandwich on the bias into spearlike slices that he arranged on three plates. He gave us cups of black coffee and, as a child of perhaps nine had materialized to run the store, the three of us moved to a table on the sidewalk.

Our baker was named Marcel and he came from a line of bakers, he said, dating back to Charlemagne. I translated with effort and clumsiness; Grace's shoulders rose. "Well, my granddaughter here is in high school. She is in *honors English*," she shouted, trying to burst through the language barrier.

He stared at me. "English classes? Why? You already speak English."

My mortification made translating more difficult. I tried to explain that I was studying literature.

"The books of the English?" He looked cut into. For a long moment, he stared off, scratching the underside of his chin. "*Quel dommage!* The English, they have no feeling for anything. What do you propose to do with yourself? How will you acquit yourself?" I had reached the outer limits of my language abilities as he raised increasingly metaphysical issues. His face darkened; he said things that I grasped at in a literal way. "Do you think life is for the clouds and the air? Life is for the blood! If you want the feeling for life, for the blood of the mind, you should be studying Hugo, Proust, Stendhal, Voltaire, Flaubert!" He turned his lecture from me to Grace. She smiled and lifted an eyebrow at me as if she understood everything and it was all satisfying. Her thoughts were written across her face: You see what can happen when you take a chance? This is what happens!

Eventually, Gram folded her napkin, telling the baker that his sandwich was "interesting": I translated this as *"superbe."* She went back inside and pointed at the glass case: This one with the chocolate shell, that one with the ganache, the baba au rhum, the one over there like a pyramid. Marcel rushed back and forth with a pair of silver tongs. "Oui, Madame; oui, Madame!" He had a wheezy, cigarette-broken laugh. Together they filled two large boxes. Then Gram simply did what she did at every shop: opened her purse full of francs and said, "Honor system." He removed one shiny, stray dime among the francs and said in English, "A memento, Madame."

We took our boxes, sagging with chocolate and cream, to a riverbank, spread our new silk scarves on the bright grass, and sat, just the two of us. The moment intertwined with the bolt of French blue sky, the warm summer air, the smell of the Seine. When we bit into them, the pastries were crisp, then bright puffs; they were clouds and bridges and fine art in gold frames and old books in leather bindings and weightless days to come.

Oh yes, I knew — *I knew, I knew!* — it was foolish to be married that first time round, for ten silly months, to Jeremy — who had lain on the couch in a haze of pot smoke and TV-lit depression and such lethargy that I found it unendurable — ending in hasty divorce, and I was so relieved to be out of it. *Still,* the idea of marriage — the comfort, the notion of certainty — had returned to enchant me once I started graduate school and took up with someone new, D. There was love, it must have been love — mustn't it?

Or maybe it was foolish to try to insist on one narrative, one easy way of interpreting such desires. D. stands for Deconstruction — his course of study in graduate school. A field filled with thickets of language. D.'s favorite theorist, Michel Foucault, said, "Maybe the target nowadays is not to discover what we are but to refuse what we are." I turned the thought over and over: If you haven't discovered who you are, can you still refuse it?

I'd walked into the seminar room and D. was long arms and legs, stretched out on a couch in the back. Hair blue-black as crows' feathers, a marvelous laugh that could get the whole room stirred up — one of the best laughers I'd ever met. D. was slumming it in a writing workshop, hiding out from the courses on postmodernism. He wrote stories about young men tormented by existential problems and by touchy young women. The class — six men, plus me — hailed his work.

One of the students said my writing, on the other hand, was "like an opera singer having a seizure." The Deconstructionist defended me vigorously, gallantly. He used the word *wonderful*. A week later, he gave me a lift home. I leaned across the front seat and experimentally nosed his ear. He was safe, both hands glued to the wheel, eyes on the highway.

"I love a man driving," I'd said.

His profile smiled. "Do that again. With your nose."

D. came to my parents' house for dinner. He brought a bottle of araq for my father. Bud served him stuffed squash and cabbage leaves. That was the first visit. After a few more such meals, Bud began his program of systematic, low-grade harassment. As Mom picked up the platters from dinner, my father rolled forward on his elbows and asked him, "So, you have intentions?"

"I've got all kinds of intentions," D.

laughed.

"The kind of getting married."

"Ohhhh . . . that kind." He sat back, offering a Mona Lisa smile.

Bud's chin was pulled in, his brows heavy: Dad with his propriety, his air of bruised dignity, indignant at Americans and their jokey ways. An Arab man with three smiling American daughters. D. was nothing if not a charming troublemaker. Bud turned his head to one side and aimed his eyes at me. "What is this? What is going on here?"

My palms felt damp. "What is what?"

"He comes to dinner fifty million times and you're not getting married?"

"Oh, no, no — I never said *that,*" D. said smoothly. "Maybe we will get married."

"When?"

"Well . . . ," D.'s eyes traveled to mine. "Eventually. Someday. Maybe."

"Someday? Maybe? What does that mean?"

"Dad, we haven't even discussed it ourselves," I broke in, enervated by a sense of déjà vu, annoyed with myself for not seeing this coming. I'd invited D. to dinner so casually, trying to prove something to myself — about my family's new openness and Americanness. I was an idiot. "We don't know what we want to do yet. If we want to

57

do *any*thing."

Bud swiveled toward me. "If you don't know, then maybe this isn't the right one for you! Maybe not! Did you think of that ever?"

After each dinner, D. and I had our post-Bud fight. We barely pulled out of the driveway and the question would burst from me, "Well, why *don't* you want to get married?" On the outside, I looked just as American as anyone, but the Jordanian daughter emerged from within, addled by a thousand years of Bedouin etiquette and advice.

Foucault said, "Where there is power, there is resistance." D. was not thrilled about the whole marriage proposition. His father had lived in the basement of their house for years, leaving an arctic region between himself and D.'s mother. I could understand his anxiety, completely empathize with it, and his reluctance made it irresistible to me.

"This is what happens when you *wish*," she says, pointing to the girl at her feet. "God plays a joke." Sitt Abdo is my grandmother's cousin. She has withered cheeks and three furrows like arrows pointing to the center of her chest. The front of her shift slips enough so I can see them, creases deep enough for a baby's finger. "All my life I wish for a child, I wish for a child. No baby, no baby. Then he plays his joke." She looks impossibly old to me when I am seven — the same age as her daughter Joumana. It is possible that she is one hundred, though I hear my aunties, later, telling each other that she is sixty-two.

Sitt Abdo, her husband Sayed Abdo, and Joumana live in the most beautiful house with whitewashed walls and rooms rippling with light, just as if someone tossed buckets of water through the air every morning and left behind sheets of brightness. As her mother carries on, Joumana looks at me with round eyes and a droll smile, so I could almost believe she is in on the joke. Her mother sighs and groans and wanders around the house in bare, lovely feet, carrying a bowl of Seville oranges. "He waits!" Sitt Abdo turns to me suddenly, as if I too played some part in the joke. "He waits until it's too late. When I'm so old I can barely see and my neck looks like a camel's back," she says, pointing to her straight spine. "And my husband is himself a three-year-old child," she throws in irritably. "When I've given up and I don't want it any longer, *that's* when God grants the wish."

Finally, Sitt Abdo lowers herself onto the step out front, muttering variations of the same thing. She puts her head down into her hand as if she's only now found out she has a seven-year-old. Joumana and I sit with her on the wide step and begin peeling the tiny, tart fruit. In a bid to regain his country, to raise his daughters to be who they were "meant" to be, Bud moved us back to Jordan months ago — a relocation that wouldn't last a year — and since we arrived, every day something surprising happens. Like this trip to Bethlehem to see Joumana.

"Don't worry," Joumana says to me, right in front of her mother. "She loves to yell."

Without saying a word, using just her fingertips, Sitt Abdo peels the hair-fine membrane from an orange segment, then touches her daughter's lips and places the fruit in her mouth.

In a few days, we take the wheezing rental car across expanses of sand and road back to Jordan. Aunt Aya greets us as though we've escaped from a live volcano. Sitting on an embroidered couch, my auntie asks for an accounting of our visit. When I tell her about Sitt Abdo, she rocks with laughter, eyes sparkling, black wings drawn at each corner. Finally, she wipes her eyes carefully and says, "That woman was born with a mouth full of complaints. Listen, *habibti* [my darling]. There are two people who can stop you from getting what you want — the person outside of you and the person inside of you. Guess which is more powerful?"

My aunt is full of tricks and puzzles: I get nothing right, but she keeps trying. Tied back with a silk Hermès scarf, her long hair is black and smooth and perfect as glass: I want to touch it, but I'm afraid of my aunt. I sit on my hands, trying to think of a good answer. After a long time, I declare, "The person outside of you!"

My aunt's lips pucker. I know she's wondering why she keeps trying. She has at least thirty-four other nieces and nephews. She says, "The one *inside, ya Salteeya* [thick-headed woman from al-Salt]."

Ohh! I roll my eyes and nod: that was what I'd *meant* to say! But at seven, all I know is my parents telling me day and night all the things I'm not allowed to do — which is everything. No standing on the table, no experimenting with the perfume, no eating the candy from between the cushions. When I grow up, I want to be a writer, like my Aunt Rachel, and tell stories like everyone in the family, and people will listen like nobody in the family. Also, I want to be constantly on an airplane, because nothing fills the air with more exciting feelings, nothing lights my parents up more than when we're on a plane pointed either to Jordan or back to the States. When we get to either place, the lovely feelings go away, but in the air, things are very good.

I try to explain this to my aunt: airplanes, silk scarves, black hair, travel, writing, excitation.

"So you want to be rich." Aya gives me a long, pleased look. "And free."

"No. Just write and fly."

She sighs, slinging one leg over the other, and bangs a cigarette out of a pack. "People don't know what they should want. They think they do, but they don't."

"Not even me?"

She smiles so widely I can see the glint of her gold tooth. My aunt gives me so much advice you'd think there was something wrong with me. That I am one big walking problem. But I'm fine! I keep trying to tell her. Even so, she slips the cigarette behind her ear, stretches her arms wide, silk sleeves unfurling like Dracula's cape, and folds me into a jasmine cloud. She whispers in my ear, "*Habibti*, especially not you."

With luck, a writer may have many chances, many fields to play in. You start out with one sort of plan for how this or that story will go; along the way, however, it forks, doubles back. If you're easy about it, you learn to follow the tales instead of the other way around: Let the work take the lead and find out what sort of writer you are.

Toward the end of my graduate work, I'd run out of funding and was eyeing help-wanted ads for fast-food "associates." After years of studying literature, I qualified for nothing in the working world. So I dedicated my free time to writing a romance novel.

Every English grad I talked to had heard of someone, somewhere, who'd paid for school by writing romances. Uncle Hal had given me a cache of garage-sale paperbacks: I pulled them out and read one a night, charting the plots and working on my own by day. I thought if I could nail down the formula, it just might sell. After a month and a half, I sent a story about a lovelorn composition instructor who's tempted by a glowering Dean of Students to a post office box at Harlequin. A week later, a kindly editorial assistant wrote to say my romance novel was too clichéd.

Next, I spotted an ad on the back page of *The Village Voice*. A "New York–based publisher seeks authors to write books." Buried deeper in the ad was a note that this was a publisher of "Adult Fiction." I assumed this was to distinguish their books from the "Young Adult" genre. My friend Liza cleared things up: "*Adult* means porn." She pushed her dark hair away from her face. "Dirty stories — the stuff they publish in *Penthouse Forum.* Not American Modernism."

"They specialize in pornography?" I propped my elbows back on the library lounge step and contemplated this. We were on a "smoking break," in which Liza smoked and I ate vending-machine candy. Over the past three years, I'd grown to enjoy inhaling her secondhand smoke, its smell a Pavlovian bell that it was time to eat a Three Musketeers.

" 'Specialize'?" Liza had a real figure and dark Mediterranean-Jewish features that made people think, of the two of us, she was the Arab. "More like — that's all they do." She exhaled a stream of smoke. "I doubt, like, they're publishing epic poetry on the side."

The raciest thing I'd ever read was snippets of my aunt's copy of James Baldwin's *Go Tell It on the Mountain,* which required hanging around in their upstairs bathroom at fourteen, gaping at the sexual coming of age of a young gay man. That afternoon, I steeled myself and called the number in the paper. Talking quickly, I assured the man who answered that I knew adult fiction "inside and out." The man, who asked me to call him "Big Al," said if my work proved satisfactory, they'd start me writing in the One-A category, or what they liked to refer to as "Missionary Position." "It doesn't pay great," Big Al added. "I tell my people, think of this as a writing workshop."

It was June, but the old mountain ridges around Binghamton were still ridged with snow, the air shining cold. Liza and I paced Front Street in front of the adult bookstore, hands deep in pockets, eyes fixed on the ice-gray sidewalk, scaring away customers. I wanted to go home, but Liza was determined. "This is too stupid. I'm going in." She pushed through the unmarked black door. A few minutes later, she burst out with a brown paper sack like a grocery bag, eyes wide. "I can't believe I did that." We scurried up frost-streaked pavement. "Only for you would I do this." She handed over a stack of paperbacks. "They had a whole wall, and a sign that said 'Literature.' " She fished a wrinkled cigarette out of her purse, smoothed it between two fingers. "Love to attend a seminar on that literature."

Big Al had recommended that I "study

up" on the genre. I read the books in a few nights: None were longer than 120 pages; the covers were thin, they curled softly — maybe intended for holding in one hand. As with the romance novels, each of these books had essentially the same plot. In this case, a good-looking man — sailor, salesman, garage mechanic — was constantly running into voluptuous goddesses. Within the first two pages, clothing melted away. Nothing to it! Such fluffy, paint-by-numbers stuff, it wasn't even shocking. There was one bit of stylistic flair: the zesty references to genitalia. I started jotting down words, noting that they generally fell into two categories. In one column, descriptors like *hot, meaty, spicy, raging,* in the other column, nouns like *staff, rod, wand, poker,* etc. You could attach any of the words in column A to any of the words in column B and make a porno anagram.

My dissertation was going to be a collection of interlinking short stories modeled after the structure of Faulkner's *Absalom, Absalom!* But first came *The Adventures of Wee Willie.* I worked and ate all meals straight from the fridge, salami, chips, grapes. Liza came over to read my latest pages, marveling, "It seems like you know how to write this."

■ ■ ■ ■

One day I got a call from Zora Minske, a graduate student in women's studies: one of my short stories — a tale about a man who constructs wings out of beer can pull tabs and flies away from his overbearing wife — had been published by *MSS,* John Gardner's literary journal, and her reading group, a high-profile cabal on campus, had decided to discuss the story at their next meeting. She hoped I might like to attend. Intimidated, I yelped, "Sure!" That night I laid stock still in bed, filled with fear and regret.

Dominated by a rectangular table, the meeting room overlooked campus and the distant blue ranges. 1986, and the women around the table in their flowing skirts were unshaven, nonwaxed, bra-free, clear of makeup or other oppressions. I was in jeans, T-shirt, and high-top sneakers. Having convinced myself that this event might involve some kind of potluck, I brought a puree of roasted eggplant with garlic and lemon, loaves of pita, and cookies. Bribes.

A few of the women smiled, eyes glittering. Silence settled in the air like smoke. One raised her brows as I uncovered the tubs. "I'm sorry, no. I have allergies."

Someone dressed in dark purple moved the dishes to a table behind a podium. The handful of women there had started discussing my story before I'd arrived. Zora, the organizer, didn't acknowledge my entrance but sat with elbows on the table, hands plunged into her hair. She looked bored and irritated, as if she wanted to be there about as much as I did. As I sat, Penny, the purple-clad student, said, "This is a vital narrative of the masculine body. The narrator an embodiment of the male gaze."

"No, no, no," Zora countered. "This text subverts the dominant paradigm by deliberately co-opting the plot, making it into a feminine journey."

Another young woman sat across from Penny, shaking her head so her springy coils of hair trembled. "Yet another good old boy's study — a guy hero — lousy wife. He's the one who gets everything — it replays all the old stories."

"So, unless a story is promoting heroic women it's not worthwhile?" Zora asked.

Penny considered the question as she strolled to the front of the room, back straight, covered with a sheath of hair, and returns with a plate of eggplant dip, bread, and cookies. "It's not a level playing field — we can't afford to have women writers idealizing male protagonists."

"There are responsibilities. There are social obligations." The woman with allergies extended one finger, pointing. "She brought food — a display of domestic labor, if you need it spelled out. It's like a billboard for women's objectification."

Most of the meeting went like this. It was too stressful to listen closely. Instead, as they toiled on, I started thinking about the growing stack of *The Adventures of Wee Willie* manuscript pages on my desk at home, right out in the open. I began to distract myself by wondering what might happen if any of these women should happen to enter my house and pass by my desk.

"Is this — eggplants?" A comp lit student named Paola interrupted, holding up a wedge of pita with a swirl of the dip on it. She took another bite. "I don't even like eggplants."

"My *point* here," skinny allergy girl said, "is that this piece doesn't give the slightest thought to the empowerment of women."

"How is this creamy like this?" Paola asked, wiping her plate with bread.

"Come over any time," I blurted, hoping we could wrap things up. "I can show you —"

"Can we not talk about food?" Skinny

glared around the table.

"A text in which there is a single, unified, male heroic figure, on a quest for gratification, is by its very construction a phallocentric entity," Penny declared, leaning against the table, exhausted.

Afterward, rising from the table, my legs felt deboned. Zora clapped me on the back. "You survived." Out of everything said that day, that was the bit that got to me — a fishhook under the skin. Maybe that was her intention. For the next three weeks, I sweated and sighed through three more meetings. Having pureed my story, they moved on to new writers and topics: patriarchal authority, the male gaze, the imprisonment of the eroticized concubine. Each night I went home and wrote more adventures for Wee Willie. I woke sweating from nightmares that I'd handed out pages to the women's studies group. In my dream I saw the paper in their hands; I tried to snatch it back; I saw women turning, horrified, faces curdled. I rose from the seminar table, stammering: No, not mine, not mine. . . .

The dream was like one long anxiety session about discovery. The meetings were a crucible of sorts. These women were authoritarian, but also serious readers — my first taste of an audience. I wanted their respect yet couldn't live up to their expectations.

"Maybe you're having an identity crisis," Liza said, an arm hooked over the back of her chair at the kitchen table. I was cracking eggs into hot linguine; lately, all I wanted was pad Thai. The recipe arrived in my grandmother's weekly stream of magazine and newspaper clippings, along with her usual blue ballpoint notations in the margins. "Sounds spicy! Too strange?"

"You're pretending to be this big feminist," she drawled. "You really don't care about any of it."

"I do so." I put my hands on my hips. That's all I could think of to say.

"What're you going to do when women's studies finds out about Wee Willie and his adventures?"

"They wouldn't even blink. They'd think it was a pedagogical device or something ironic or — like, Madonna." I shrugged one-shouldered, twirled noodles. "And they are never going to find out."

Liza gave me a dead-eye glance, her irises nearly as dark as her pupils. "You should decide if you want to be a writer or what the hell."

It occurred to me, with a mild burst of happiness, that I didn't have to keep going to women's studies meetings. Instead, I

71

stayed home and put Wee Willie through his paces. A bumbling traveling salesman, shy and retiring, who happens to be ridiculously well endowed, Willie's true desire is to sell his top-notch, Swiss-made vacuums. The neighborhood ladies are lonely, libidinous souls who prey on Willie. Night after night, I lived on coffee and chocolate chip cookies, hunched before my hulking computer monitor, grinning, scribbling Willie's story, my thesis sleeping under my desk.

I slid a sheath of pages into an envelope and shipped it out.

Several days later, at home, staring at my unfinished thesis, I heard a knock downstairs. In a scene straight out of my recurring nightmares, my housemate Meryl pounded up the stairs to say that "two scary girls" were there. Zora and Penny from women's studies.

"You haven't been at meetings," Zora said, cranky as ever.

"We wanted to say hi." Penny smirked. She was the kind of friend, my Uncle Hal would have said, you couldn't stop hugging for fear they'd strangle you. Certain I had to have been ill to miss a meeting, they had brought a small bag of brown leaves and twigs they'd bought from the Chinese herbalist store downtown. It had a high mushroomy reek, like that of the herbal remedies my aunt smuggled through customs.

"Come in," I managed. "Wow. My gosh, you guys. How great is this."

They trooped up the many flights of stairs into our shared dollhouse, complimenting everything. Penny lingered over my pink-shag-rug bedspread and Talking Heads poster; the built-in bookshelves in the hallway; the scorched pots hanging over the stove. I let them peek into our few rooms, then led them out the back door. For a while, we stood on the landing overlooking dripping clotheslines, watching Zora smoke. My guilty old conscience flared — I felt caught — half truant and half escapee. I babbled about how crazy-busy I'd been, supposedly laboring on my thesis.

Gradually, though, I calmed down: It dawned on me they weren't on some reconnaissance mission, they really just came over — the way people did in graduate school. I pulled myself together and let them back inside. Feeling expansive, I settled them in our two beanbag chairs in the living room. My housemate drifted through, giving everyone a wide berth.

In the kitchen, I rattled around fixing twig

tea, looking for healthy things to offer them. Which was when I realized the answering machine had clicked on. The phone ringer in our apartment had been permanently disabled by a downstairs landlord, so the only way we knew someone was calling was when a disembodied voice shouted in the hallway and everyone jumped out of their skin. I hurried into the living room, tea ball in one hand:

"Diana? Big Al. Got your work. It's quality. We can't go with the name Wee Willie, though. How about Steve? Also, listen, you got to slow it down — I mean the pace, babe. You're gonna burn out. He can't be pumping on every page. Take it down a click. Anyway, I love it. Send me the next story by next Friday and you'll get a bonus. Over and out."

I was flash frozen. I couldn't look at Zora or Penny. Of course this had to happen. I'd smugly decided I was safe. It's always the thing you think can't possibly happen. I'd sent Wee Willie out a week ago, filed or scrapped any remaining evidence of writing, hidden the dirty-book "research" in a shoe box under the bed. I thought: This is what happens when you try to keep secrets! Excuses flew through my head. Confess, I thought. Tell them the truth: you needed the money.

Zora made a little breath sound, a half-cough, and said, "Was that a publisher?" Penny's smirk faded. Here I was, getting calls at home from an important person.

"Oh gosh," I stammered. "It's — no. It's not anything. Just a little — I don't know. I'm working on something — on the side. It's not academic, it's — for fun." I half-shrugged, squeezed the fingers of one hand in the other. I heard Penny exhale. "Just — wow."

I saved this message and for months to come I played Big Al back to dinner-party guests. I told them, "Oh, he's this publisher who can't get enough of my work." When I came clean about his specialty, people wanted to hear the message again and again.

Al was right: I couldn't stand the pressure. I was pleased to collect my check for $900 and tell him that was the end. Writing was hard enough: I had to feel easy about the way I approached it.

I never saw the actual book, *The Adventures of Big Steve,* which was just as well — I would've had to hide it. Despite having been married and divorced, I'd returned to a virginal state as far as my father was concerned. You peel away one code, one restriction, and find another just under-

75

neath. Good daughters didn't get divorced, and underlying this — they didn't have sex — certainly not without producing babies; they didn't know about it; they certainly didn't write books about it. Sex was something for wild American girls.

The end of grad school brought everything into sharp relief: I was offered a teaching position in Lincoln, Nebraska, and then D. was offered a scholarship to spend a semester studying in Paris. When D. received word of his award, he came home waving the letter jubilantly, drunk with excitement, and blurted out, "Let's get married, too!"

Some native sense in me crept back. He would go read books in Paris and I would go . . . teach freshman composition in Nebraska? But my ancestors' collective insistence on marriage was always there: it lapped at my dreams, whispered behind my head. I was stubborn and indoctrinated. I threw my arms around his neck.

The second wedding was as low-key as the first was elaborate: no parents allowed — due to lingering grudges nursed by certain parties. We held it in our apartment, performed by a justice plucked from the Yellow Pages. Afterward, a dinner for eighteen friends at the only place with a big enough table to fit our party. There was a chocolate cake some friends had iced with the words: "You should only live long and be happy." The previous night, three girlfriends had taken me out in a convertible and we'd sung, *I only have eyes for you, dear* . . . flinging the words into the soft, black air.

Months later, I went off to Paris to visit my new husband in the Algerian–Moroccan neighborhood called the Marais. In a flat as squat and ugly as a cinderblock, D. had one square window that swung open to gray sky and clotheslines. There was a cement shelf outside under the windowpane where he kept bread, cheese, and milk. I ate a few bites, absorbed by how delicious everything was. A croissant and a thin tablet of black chocolate loosened my senses. And yet the man I was visiting looked starved. When I first walked off the plane, I didn't recognize his face so much as the way he was standing, curving forward as if about to catch something. D. was thin, his skin and teeth pearlescent. When I put my arms around him, I could feel the bones in his back. "Are you — how are you?" I said, aghast.

"I forgot how beautiful you are." He kissed my head; his favorite spot — he called this a "righteous kiss."

I kept glancing at him, but it seemed plain

that I wasn't meant to ask about this transformation. There was a new, furtive air about him, as if he were keeping a secret.

The miserable room came with some meals. D. left early in the morning to go to class, but he had conserved half his breakfast for me: a basket with a feathery croissant, a bowl of blackberry preserves, a sweet orange, a square of something halfway between an excellent cheese and butter, a cup of strong black coffee, half a pitcher of yellow cream. I ate slowly. A commotion of doves outside brought me to the window that framed a view of narrow, sooty streets, pitched roofs, clotheslines, pinched and crowded and charming. The light was so crisp and starched the room seemed almost quaint. The coffee was rich: my body awakened with a sip.

Before his departure overseas we'd had a few moony weeks that were actually delightful, our imminent separation making everything lovely and doomed. We'd kissed with a heat I hadn't felt in the past three years. But after we'd been apart for a few months with little communication, I struggled to remember what D. looked like. In Lincoln, a naturalist in pointed boots and worn jeans started to court me. He didn't write and he didn't know anything about critical theory.

After weeks of pursuit during which I asserted I was married and the naturalist asserted I wasn't, we kissed in his double-wide trailer till we were shaking and then laughed at ourselves. Later, we stood outside the trailer in the frigid night, examining constellations, the smear of the Milky Way, the stars so clear they looked close enough to prick a finger.

When I thought about D., I heard his loud laugh, remembered that he loved film and golf and wine and food. My memory had brought up nothing like this monkish, self-mortifying figure. D. seemed transformed by Paris, reading Proust in French, studying the lives of saints, scholars, philosophers, men who evidently believed that illumination came through self-denial, that a mind that eclipses the body burns more brightly. Each morning he beetled off to class and didn't return until almost bedtime. After a week of this un-reunion, I was thinking about flying home early when I discovered a notebook under the bed. In it, D. described in semi-coded language an ongoing affair with a charming young language professor.

Though I'd already half-guessed it, was already half-involved with someone else myself, I felt clobbered, a frying pan to the gut. Breathless, I kicked the notebook back under the bed, then I kicked the bed too, the iron bedstead smashing my sneaker. Good! As I grabbed my foot, my eyes flooded with angry tears. I bitterly considered the kiss on my head: the only one I'd received since arriving. The righteous kiss was the last Romeo gave to Juliet — his farewell. D. had kissed me this way for ages, which I saw now as years of goodbyes. After I'd sat with these thoughts for a while, I felt a whisper of unsettling emotions. I thought I must be dizzy or in shock. I went outside, crossed the boulevards. The men and women clipping by in dark suits looked like pieces across a chessboard, their faces revealing nothing. It was late fall, days before Thanksgiving in the States. Winter seemed to be arriving in high, invisible clouds, round scrolls releasing the cold. All of this suited my mood — I was glad to feel lonely and misunderstood. The more I thought about it, the more I began to feel certain we'd married for the worst possible reasons — to be secure, to please others — and so there had ensued betrayals and affairs and separations. Now I saw it clearly written out in D.'s tidy block print, the same printing he used in the margins of his books. The internal workings of our relationship, intimate, physical, whatever there was, had started to collapse.

That afternoon, I sat through a mass at a chapel on the Rue *X,* trying to feel something other than relief. Blame flitted here and there, a sparrow in the rafters. I watched the priest lift the host, vestments rippling down his arms; there was a catch in my chest. I had the sense that, for all my family's warnings and advice, I wasn't ready to be in love with anyone. It seemed that all advice could do was separate you from your own voice, the one that tells you to wait for what you want — that someday, not yet, desire will be there, buzzing in the trees, ready for you to look up. I sighed and felt sorry for myself. Also a little hungry. The hymns and stained glass and ceremony were such an astringent kind of loveliness, cold and airy and distant.

It was even colder outside when I left the church; frosted leaves rattled, sweeping the sidewalks. I ducked into another café, shivering so much the waiter brought me a hot cocoa before I ordered. He placed it on the table. *"Ici."* I cradled it in both hands, the brew as strong as coffee, so intense it woke me up. I looked at my own dark, liquid dreams. I'd imagined a joyous reunion: a love affair conducted on the city bridges.

And when I tried to picture the face of the one I loved, there was nothing. I drank two more cups of that chocolate, watching tourists hustle up the boulevard, their coats belled before them, full of wind.

To fall out of love while continuing to love — just not in that way — is like the reverse of an arranged marriage, in which strangers are able, over time, to fall passionately in love. D. and I reunited after his term in Paris. There was no throwing of dishes, but there was some lively discussion of what it meant to fall in love with other people, how it was, perhaps, not conducive to a marriage — or at least not the sort we might have hoped for. In a few rare, honest moments, I glimpsed the swap that I'd made in my marriages — freedom from my father's rule in exchange for giving up on desire. Then I assured myself that couldn't be it — okay, well, the first time, yes — but surely the second was for love. Still, we never again reached for each other; our contact shrank to holding hands. D. and I lived in a sort of cascade of disintegration, neither of us able to look at it directly. We went to films in basement theatres, sprinkled truffle oil on the pasta, talked to each other late into the evenings — as friends, such good, old friends. It seemed at times, in our chaste bed, that friendship was enough to make a marriage. For five years, I missed desire, but not that much. Mostly the idea of it.

We taught, we moved and moved. We talked about houses and babies — as though describing a life built together was the same as having one. Then I applied for my own travel grant.

When we first arrived in Jordan, where I would spend a year writing in the capital city of Amman, D. and I passed our days with friends, driving to ruins and monuments, taking walks that spiraled along the cobbled streets and broken sidewalks, sampling street kabobs and sipping coffee, going drinking and dancing, attending parties in emptied buildings where, at some point, someone would pull out a pistol and shoot at the moon. Occasionally I sat at my desk and stared at the notes for my novel, clutching my hair, not seeing any way out. Then very quickly it was spring break in Jordan, just like in the States, and everyone goes away to somewhere. Istanbul is popular, but my friend Mai proposed a group trip to Cairo. It would be she and Armand and D. and I. We would stay at a large Western-style hotel on Zamalek, the flower-bound island in the center of the city. D. and I had to produce a wedding license — which the hotel takes and stores in a safe — in order to stay in the same room. Mai and Armand each had their own rooms.

At night, I sense footsteps in the hotel corridor past our door, the furtive pressures of embraces and release just beyond the thin wall. They don't make a sound.

It's so hot in Cairo that Mai and I dry our hands on our hair in restrooms, the sweat in our clothes dries on our backs. We gaze at the Sphinx and the pyramids through an iridescence of sand; we try to ignore the streams of importuning young Egyptians.

"What time is it, Miss Americans?"

"Hello, hello, how are you? How do you do?"

"You need a guide? I am yours."

"Idiots. Comedians," Mai mutters, though more gently than usual. "No wonder they'll never get anywhere." Armand makes a diplomatic calming motion, gathering the tips of his fingers, but Mai doesn't look at him. "Why should I be quiet? They think if you say it in English it doesn't count."

At night, the lovely hotel waits and sighs around us. D. sits at the edge of our bed and watches the news in an unfamiliar language. Perversely, I make my lists:

Sophie, Iris, Kalani. Because you want the thing you can't have; you want it the most. I first started making these lists in the fall, around the time we arrived in Jordan. Camille, Daphne, Maya. Girls' names, since it was all fantasy anyway. My grandmother had passed away three years earlier. I write Grace at the top of each list.

The future is pressing against us. Mai is thirty-two, I'm thirty-three. We don't speak openly to each other about our dearest hopes. Jordanians, like many non-Americans, have a reserve about their private lives so ingrained it can seem at times like a form of self-preservation. When the Egyptians ask us about who we are and where we come from, Mai responds in a hearty voice, *"Ehna Salteeyeen!"* We are from Al-Salt! Ancient village of our big, bossy families, a place famous, some say, for stubbornness and for difficult women. It breaks them up, these thin, kohl-eyed people so ready for a laugh. That's the most we will reveal to the Cairenes. Mai would perhaps be horrified that I am writing these lines about her, this story. I hope for her blessing.

I love Mai most of all for her serrated edge, her impatience, her dignity. She was born this way, with this beautiful, aloof face, her toasted-biscuit color, her eyes like tinted windows. Men are drawn to her, then disconcerted by her manner. We walk through the Khan el-Khalili souq, unanswered wishes weighing us down. I want something permissible yet somehow unattainable, Mai wants something attainable yet not permitted. She is silently in love with Armand. They work together in separate governmental agencies and are fast friends, but there isn't a whiff of romance about them. Our friend Dobb tells me more: Armand is married, and although he and his wife have been separated for years, they are Italian Catholics and refuse to divorce. Adding to these difficulties, Mai is Muslim and won't marry outside of her religion. All of the members of this play seem frozen in place, bound by social dictums and family pressures.

"It's absurd," I complain to Dobb. "They're in love — that's what matters."

Dobb, a twenty-four-year-old gay Armenian-Christian in Jordan, raises his eyebrows discreetly. "A person can choose to feel however they need to feel."

"No, you can't!"

He smirks. "You sound exactly like an American."

This kind of desire isn't permitted to a

86

well-brought-up Jordanian girl. The Qur'an says:

> Have you seen the one who has chosen his own desire as his lord? God has knowingly caused him to go astray, sealed his ears and heart and veiled his vision. Who besides God can guide him?

The talented Egyptian dancers know how to whirl desire over the expanse of the belly, to swirl it in midair. But the good Jordanian girl must live in the ellipses between *ibe* (shame) and *haram* (taboo). The Jordanian girl must move rapidly — from her father's house to her husband's, with no funny business in between — if she is ever to move at all. The babies will be the recipients of maternal ardor, the doting gaze a white light upon their limbs. Before marriage, Bud allowed us a little more ambition than that — instead of eros, we might have education or work. We might listen to his recordings of the great Egyptian singer Umm Kulthum swooning over her unnameable love. We might learn how to twine snake arms overhead, how to lift and drop each hip, to make a belt of coins ring with each kick. There were always the fine distractions of music, or dancing, or visiting, or food; sheets of filo dough, buttered and anointed with syrup, nearly enough to compete with a night in bed.

In a tiny café, I sit beaming below an oil portrait of Naguib Mahfouz: Beside me, Mai doesn't smile as the waiter snaps our picture.

Both D. and I can see that Mai and Armand are consumed by each other, which might in turn make us a little wistful, feeling the contrast. Only when I see such couples do I feel the edge of what's missing, the slim blade of the possible and the denied. Though of course none of us express our dangerous thoughts. During the day, they are the very image of opprobrium, scarcely looking in each other's direction, but they're sweetened by a residue from the nights. Perhaps Mai and Armand can sense there is something stopped or canceled between me and D., but if so, they don't let on. Our secrets are shared yet not spoken. I try to remember how or when D. and I stopped touching each other, but there's no single day, no critical moment to point to. Even when we were young animals, it seems we lived so much in our minds, hearts in cages. There was sex and there was us, a quiet, still zone in between.

On our last day in Cairo, we ask the concierge to take our picture as a group, then we forget the camera on the shuttle bus to the airport. Once at the departure gate, chill descends: Mai arranges that she and I will board in advance of the men. We sit in the eighth row, Armand in the forty-second. We return to lives of friendly distance. I'd hoped that whatever had been set in motion between Mai and Armand in Cairo might come back with them, some embers, crackling at the edges. But fire needs to breathe — they'd made their secret airtight.

That fall, after nine years of marriage, barely a month after D. and I return to the States, unaccountably, I begin giving away clothes. I box my belongings — books, artwork, pots and pans — and offer them to people. I feel compelled to do it: It's a rush of light and energy, as if I'm increasing freedom with each donation. One morning, I fit my remaining stuff into a few suitcases and some book boxes. It all seems more haphazard than deliberate: I don't have a plan. I bike around the park blocks near the Portland State campus where I teach, a ruffled, leafy area. An apartment building outfitted with blue awnings catches my eye. The young woman in the front office leads me down the hall, keys jingling, warning, "Now, it's tiny." The first thing I see is gray brilliance: The Willamette River shines like nickel through the panes.

Of course, I put off telling them.

Weeks go by, then more weeks. I don't know how to admit to this much failure and I'm afraid of their reaction. When my parents call, D. is "napping," or he "just ran out." Frequently, he's "in the shower. He says hi." Suddenly, three months have passed: Every couple of days I drive to our old apartment to check the mail rather than confess to a new address. For a while, I imagine that not telling is actually my way of being boldly independent . . . until all at once it just seems like cowardice. I pick up the phone, try to piece words together. I put the phone down. In desperation, I sit before the computer. I write, "So guys, hey, sorry to do this by email, but I've been meaning to tell you a little something. . . ."

Mom writes back, "Yeah, we didn't think he took that many showers."

Two minutes after Mom's response, Bud calls. "You want me I should round up the boys, go pay the *kelb* a visit?" He's offering to beat my ex, *the dog,* no questions asked

— but he puts it in an affable, conversational way.

"Bud. It's fine. Things just — they weren't right. For a really long time. We just didn't. . . ."

"What? What didn't you?"

I fish for the words, searching the air. "It's hard to really —"

"Did he beat you?" Bud still suspects (incorrectly) that the first *kelb* beat me.

"Dad," I sigh. I can't think of any way to explain this that he could really get his head around. I hardly understand it myself. "No, Dad."

"Not a little?"

"No."

"I never trusted him," he says (a lie). "He didn't like to sit and talk to me. Not for more than an hour or two." Here is my father's best, truest test of character: who is willing to spend days at a time, without cease, talking to him? That is the person who can be trusted.

"No, Bud, you were right."

"If only you will listen." Now he sighs.

"If only."

Three years earlier, my grandmother had spent her final days in a hospital bed. We'd returned to written messages, our old form of communication, since she'd had thyroid

91

surgery, her neck too swollen for speech. These notes between us seemed like quiet last words, though none of us acknowledged this. She bent over a notepad, then showed us her lovely penmanship saying how happy she was that my sisters and I were "settled" and "squared away." I'm not sure she imagined that any of us difficult, untamable girls actually wanted to be married, but she would have felt sorry about losing D. Over the years, she'd knitted him several immense pullovers that he dutifully sweated into each time we visited her. A few months before anyone knew she was sick, we'd gone to a family dinner. D. sat on her left and treated her to his rolling laugh as she told him scandalous family stories about Aunt Myrtle, Father Liam, and the mystery baby — my cousin Padraic — or the three bachelor uncles who shared a bed but weren't actually brothers. Listening well was another of his virtues. Afterward, he could recount hair-raising things about my extended family — including the backstory of the cousin who'd claimed to be a prophet and kickstarted his own cult — that I'd never heard before.

But I'd imagine Grace would've been as philosophical about my second split as she was about the first. Among her many brothers and sisters, she was the only one to spend most of her life single; this, she swore, was the key to happiness. After my first divorce, she'd said, merely, "Well, I'm just glad you got that out of your system."

Two years after I left Jordan, Mai was diagnosed with a monstrous, nearly unknown form of cancer: It sprang, seemingly, from nowhere, leeching the life force from her blood. She came to the States seeking medical attention. Still exquisite, aloof, and tanned, she looked not at all sick.

I have started seeing someone new: Mai likes him. He slips an arm around my waist and I think I see the wistfulness on her face that I'd felt in Cairo. When it's time for her to return to Jordan, she clings to my shoulders and whispers in my ear, "I'm so scared."

That would be the last time I saw Mai. I learned of her death through friends of friends, weeks after the funeral near her parents' home in Al-Salt.

There is something I think I couldn't quite get until I was a bit older, which is that there are unique configurations of time and people. They belong to each other for a while, months or years, atoms in a crystal, until eventually, bit by bit, they fall away.

That's the part a younger person doesn't believe — that it won't last forever, that this assortment will never come together again.

I see my grandmother in one of her flowing "pajama suits," seated at the restaurant table, this one oversize and rectangular, leaning into D., squeezing his elbow, the two of them laughing, coconspirators. I see Mai seated at the breakfast table beside me in Cairo, turning on her finger a gold ring, stamped with large Roman numerals, a ring I'd never seen her wear before, one that slipped, just a bit loose, the last time we saw each other.

All things in due time, my grandmother liked to say, as if eventually desires become clear, the dearest wishes rise to the surface, and all best possibilities pass through your net if you just hold it out long enough. But I began to feel that wasn't quite true, that one must swing, and swing the net high and wide. There is never enough time and the net is too small. After almost thirty-five years of family, roommates, and husbands, the move into the tiny apartment marked the first time in my life I would truly live in my own space. I'd touched the sliding glass door, the pane so thin I could feel the traffic thrum of a distant bridge along the bones in my forearm. The sense of this opening

94

out, threaded with fear, was also sharp and sure, a diamond-hard bolt: the first moment of hearing your own voice. It takes such a long time, I thought, to get to the starting place.

■ ■ ■ ■

Part II
A Food of
One's Own

■ ■ ■ ■

CHAPTER FOUR:
UNKNOWN

I'd blurted to Scott, a few months after we'd become a couple, "I really think I want to have a kid!"

He'd said, "It's nice to meet you, too."

I was testing the idea, daring myself at the same time I was daring him. Sick of ambivalence, that draining sensation, I'd waited instead for baby-fever, pictured a mistral sweeping away clouds, rotating over the desert floor, a force of intention and desire. If you wanted so badly to be a mother, perhaps that meant there was something inside, some muscle, some hidden talent, that would ensure you would make a good mother. I was thirty-six when Scott and I started dating. I knew only that I wanted to want. At last, here was someone I could imagine wanting with.

Over the course of four years, we moved in together, joined our bank accounts, bought a house. Each step made me panicky with anxiety. Especially the house. For months after we moved in, I walked around as if there were unexploded mines in the floor. I was afraid of old traps, of waking up and discovering that I'd fallen into the wrong relationship. Or gotten married. Or forgotten how to write. Over the years, several of my teachers had suggested that a writing life was a vocation, that one was called to it, that any woman who wanted to be a serious writer should consider avoiding marriage and children, become a high priestess. But when I lived alone, I mostly wanted to give dinner parties. I started writing a column for *The Oregonian* about restaurant life that required eating out and gossiping with chefs all over town. My half-finished novel waited in the corner like a troll; I made wide circles, avoiding it.

At the time I met Scott, he was working in a fly-fishing shop, tying flies, selling gear, and taking customers out to water's edge, showing them how to use the expensive stuff he'd sold them. "Fly-fishing," he'd explained to me, "is for people who are privileged enough to needlessly complicate their lives." From outdoor equipment, he went on to selling boats — then even bigger boats. A born salesman with a sharpshooter's eye, he could look into people and see what they truly wanted — or what he could convince them they wanted. By our third or fourth date, he'd said, "We have to arrange things to make it easier for you to write."

After years of stealing time, ducking out of dates with friends, putting off paper-grading or eating a proper dinner — always at war with the world and the self, forever stealing away to write — this was the relief of recognition, a kind of leavening. In an antiques/junk shop, Scott found a hulking dining-room table with fluted edges and mosaic inlay; he situated it under the window with a view of the coastal range where I could work and watch storm clouds roll in.

I went to my table early in the morning, warming my hands on a coffee mug, staring through reflections in the dark window. So good to feel in possession of yourself, thoughts moving through in glassy waves. Seven years had passed since the publication of my first novel. At my dining-room table, sheets of rain blurring the sky over Portland, I began writing a new novel. It was about an Iraqi restaurant in a mythically sunny Los Angeles. It's a fine, expectant thing to write at one's table, even if, of course, you write without hope — almost every writer I know loses faith, utterly, precipitously, in any given project, at some point or other. Sometimes you get it back, but in any case, you learn how to ignore yourself and keep going. About twenty minutes after sitting down, there would be the phone ringing, then my father's voice shouting from the other room, "Hello? *Ya Bah?*" Little Daddy. Nickname for a bossy girl. "It's just me. Your dad! You are there? Get over to the *telephona*, I got things to ask you."

Even after my two marital implosions, my father still just wanted, as he said, to make sure his girls were "situated," meaning married. I'd finally started doing things like writing books, and gradually he began to see that I might be leading a different sort of life than the one he'd envisioned. Still, as soon as Scott and I bought the house together, Bud started to go a tiny bit crazy: First, because we still weren't married, and second, because we'd bought a house without consulting him.

"Your grammy might think that's cute, but not me," Bud shouted. Grace had been dead for seven years, but they were still fighting. I got up from my table, as I did each morning, and turned down the volume on the machine to a sub-audible stream of advice. Then, a hunt through the freezer for breakfast ice cream: bowls of rocky road or chocolate with peanut butter cups, preferably capped with dollops of whipped cream. This was the subversive breakfast I'd picked up from Gram, who'd fixed us eggs, bacon, and sliced cantaloupe — but only when our parents were around. On our own, meals were kids' paradise — rivers of chocolate and cream. "My dominion, my apartment, my rules," Grace declared. "I says so."

Cool, sweet spoonfuls sliding down my throat, I wrote and rewrote. When the ice cream was gone, I went after our dog, scooping her around her skinny Italian greyhound middle and flipping her onto her back. "Be the baby," I commanded. She pulled in her bony feet and gazed at me with wet eyes. A Roman bump on her nose, lips dark as if she'd applied lipstick. When I kissed her head, she tucked the length of her muzzle under my chin, tapping cold wet under my earlobe. We walked around the kitchen like that for a while until Scott said, "Aren't you supposed to be writing?"

I let the dog escape and captured the dark-eyed man in my arms. Oh, it wasn't just that he led me back to my work — that was so much, yet possibly the least of it. There were enlaced fingers and kisses like falling from great distances and an unbroken gaze like a rope between us. Desire like this was more than discovering another body, it was discovering your own — the depth and dimensions of it. Like the dream in which you walk to the back of your house and find a hidden door that opens to a floating city of onion domes, turrets, and waterfalls. This sort of desire could almost make you sad or angry, for all that you might have gone through your life without knowing. But then you just had to feel grateful again: You didn't in any way qualify for this love, you lucked into it.

"I'm ready to read your new pages," he says into my neck, about the sexiest thing he could ever say. He's never been married and yet seems to have a shocking nonchalance about trying it out. "Soon as you're ready to show them."

"Fine," I say. "Let's do it. Marriage. Whatever. Why not."

The gazebo at the end of the pier costs a grand to reserve, or . . . the concierge cocks one eyebrow, gives a shrug of a smile.

Or?

Take a chance. No one else reserves it on whatever day you pick? You can do what you want, throw a wedding — no charge.

In September, Key West is a hot mouth.

104

Its clouds are fat-bellied, trundling just above the earth. This is our mythical place, sly and entrancing with cat shadows, blue-banded water, and nights that slide over our shoulders. After a vacation there, startling and too brief, we both thought of it for our wedding. Now there are twenty wedding guests assembled. Everyone watches the sky. "It's gonna come down." Dave, my father-in-law-to-be, shades his eyes.

Bud stands with him, filled with joy and complaint. The dads. "I dun care what it does, just as long as I dun have to get back into that *machina* that brung us here. You see that thing? I feel like I'm back in the king's air force, when I flew the airmail plane. Did I tell you about how I was flying that? I was sixteen. People kept falling out."

We'd opened wedding gifts that morning, before the ceremony, pushed by a sense of expediency — several of our older guests were already making comments about the heat, using words like "ungodly." Invisible hurricanes dot outlines on the sky, churning just beyond the horizon. No one seemed to know what to give us: We'd bought our house together three years earlier, we're too old for toasters. This gathering is more like an excuse for a vacation with nuptials thrown in. One beautifully wrapped present

105

turned out to be a weather barometer embedded in a coffee mug. My parents gave up and wrote a check. Scott's grandmother Jean gave us a battered Betty Crocker cookbook from 1967. "Was this one of your favorites?" I ask her. A few food-stained pages fall out.

"Oh, gracious no." She waves a hand at me.

"Well." I hug the book to my chest. "Thank you."

"What does this mean about babies?" Suddenly her tone is bracing, a let's-get-down-to-business whip-snap.

I sit at attention. "About . . . ?"

She lifts her gaze, regal and impatient. I catch flashes of my own grandmother in her purple lipstick, the steel in her posture. "If you're ever going to have them."

Jean stops just short of saying *tick tock.* I do a kind of mental reshuffle. The rest of our party have gone in to sweat on their beds and take third showers. The wedding is in a few hours. My future grandmother-in-law and I are lingering at one of the plastic beachside tables at the hotel, surrounded by crumpled wrapping paper and drained margarita glasses the size of fish bowls. The urge for asking advice has resurfaced in me lately. Such an ingrained impulse it's made seeing therapists almost impossible — I end up begging, "Please just tell me what to do." I know there's some kind of protocol: grow up, fall in love, get married, have babies. Roughly in that order. But I've fallen out of step. I want a village elder, a bent crone to herd me back into line. I touch her hand which is cool and puffy, her manicure fire-engine red. "It's so hard to figure out!" I cry. I have these impulses of self-revelation; they come in gusts, often with the most unsympathetic confessor. "I mean, here we are. I'm forty! I'm trying to — I don't know what I'm trying to — I'm just so unsure. I mean I think I do — want them. The babies. Then I have a heart attack about it. Wow. Then I think — you had *four* of them. And Dave — what a sweetheart he must've been. All of them. I'll bet you never regretted any of it, did you?"

Her smile is a stroke that curls up at the ends. "It's all heartache, my dear," she says. "Heartache and regret, every bit of it."

Luckily, the pier is not otherwise in use and we gather there in our wrinkled nice clothes. But it turns out that MTV is filming something called *Summer Beach House* on the sand directly behind the pier. Later, watching the wedding video, we can see our lips forming the words to our vows, but all we can hear is Bananarama singing, "It's a cruel, cruel summer." In the background, girls and boys in postage stamp–size swimwear bound past as if slowed down, gold and amber-colored flesh soaring against blue. There are no clouds over the gazebo, such bright pale sky you can see almost to Mars. The twenty-two members of our wedding party put their arms around each other and smile bravely, even defiantly, right into the light.

We fly back to our lives in the mist; after Key West, our house looks tired as a sigh, the backyard a living mass of blackberry thorns and canes. That spring, I have a job offer in Miami and we decide after a few moments of agony to leave Oregon. Craving that blue, brilliant light, we sell or give away almost everything in a blaze of energy and drive across oceans of Nebraska and Iowa to South Florida. Our new little Question, bedeviling, unanswerable, finds me again. It's as if all the old patterns had been torn away in our lives — why not try some new craziness? The wisps of feelings intensify, that quality of missing someone begins drifting over me more frequently. I debate The Question privately, brooding over it . . .

just one child. . . .

I push it away. It comes back. I raise it at dinner; Scott shakes his head. I let it go; accept it; tell myself: not for you. Once we married, even Bud turned expansive and lazy, saying things like, "Your sisters took care of having the babies for you. It's lucky!" Still, I talk it over with friends. I announce contentment: I love having my freedom! Often, though, I slip into a reverie, murmuring, *just one*. . . . An acquaintance unhappy with a lack of progress in her own writing career — her hands full with an unruly daughter — scowls when I ask how one manages both writing and kids. She scolds, "You can't have everything, you know." People question me at readings and talks: Do you have any kids? I think I detect a streak of sympathy in their eyes. One day, after giving a reading, after I'm asked yet again about kids, another woman in the audience cries out, "Her books are her children!" She's indignant, head lifted: I toss up my hands, laughing, but I don't mean it. It feels like a bit of flayed skin from my throat, the back of my laughter. I don't want books to be my children.

Whitewashed buildings stream by as we ride through the streets of Amman. I'm in Jordan with Scott to visit universities, read from the new memoir, and talk about writing. But every taxi driver squints in the rearview mirror and asks where our children are, their faces expectant and wry. After a few wrong answers, I start to say, *Inshallah* — God willing — so they nod, instead of doing what the first drivers did — stare with horror and pity. Then another driver asks, and I forget my response of convenience and answer him honestly: we don't have any.

"Why not?" The young man nearly rises out of his seat as we swerve around a traffic circle. All I can see in the mirror is a thatch of hair and smudged black eyes. The mirror keeps slipping to point at the floor; he adjusts it, aiming it at me. He speaks English but doesn't address Scott, as though he knows this situation must be my doing. "You have to. They're essential. Children are God's blessing. I myself have five. Each one is a diamond."

I feel a little hitch in my throat when he says this. Something I wish to ignore. He speaks as if meting out life's facts. His ID card, clipped to the visor, says Majed Abouzayd, and a somber face that seems at once sixteen and sixty-two stares at us from the photograph. The upholstery in this car looks like someone tried to stab it to death: There are broken crank windows on both sides, shreds hanging from the ceiling, and a reek of toasted cumin and something else, ancient and terrible, in the air. I press my hands between my knees. "They're so much work. And we're — I don't know. We're just happy with things as they are." I try to recall Scott's usual arguments, but he opts out of the conversation, glued to the side window. I know he's wondering, as he often does, about the way certain people in my family are drawn to intense conversations with strangers.

Majed smiles in the mirror, his eyes narrowing into long, dark creases: "You just don't know yet."

"No really, trust me. . . ." I'm trying to laugh as I sit forward to contradict him. But he raises two fingers, a flourish, and cuts in, saying, "You don't know what happiness is."

A few weeks later, on a plush Miami night, we're back at home, sitting outside. I wait as Scott tends the grill, like I watched my uncles when I was seven, waiting for the shish kabobs, breathing the lovely scent, the coal-hiss connected directly to hunger. There are bottles of beer with wedges of lime tucked in the necks and a tabbouleh salad with bits of parsley dark as jade. Just around this time, almost ten years ago, I touched a glass pane, looking across the Willamette River into another life. I knew something new was coming, yet I couldn't have imagined this velvety late night, couldn't have known I'd be sitting outside with a cutting board on my lap, a canopy of foxtail palms curving overhead. I rub halved garlic cloves over the toasted surfaces of sliced baguette and say to my husband, "There's a question I'd like to explore . . . a little bit." We look at each other, our expressions blurred in the dark. There's no knowing what is possible, only the willingness to take the next step, blind, into midair.

Maybe the first bits of parenting occur when you begin imagining your way into it. Or perhaps it's when the sadness of not doing it begins to shiver inside your body. Maybe it's different for everyone. I read that one of Julia Child's greatest regrets was that she'd never had children. All that lovely cooking and eating, and no child to share it with. There it is, the grief of it, clanging.

A therapist tells me with a laugh that her own daughter didn't want kids and instead offered her "grand-doggies." I can't meet her eyes.

My grandmother had been so dismissive of having children, and even so, baby pictures of me and my sisters lined her walls, black and white, the photography studio air filled with soap bubbles, our hands lifted.

Several years after our wedding, after much dithering and debate, nothing is decided, but my body begins acting independently of my mind. I drag my reluctant husband to a famous fertility doctor. The Coral Gables waiting room is filled with pregnant women, husbands escorting wives belly-first through doorways. But the doctor doesn't want forty-four-year-old eggs. He conducts his examination and pronounces me fit — as a vessel. "Great! We'll give you hormonal injections, trick your body into thinking it's pregnant, and select an egg donor."

"You mean — someone else's baby?"

His eyes flutter slightly. "Somebody else's *egg*. DNA can come from your husband and half will come from — you know, elsewhere. We'll dig up a donor who looks like you, talks like you, thinks like you. You'll give birth to a gorgeous, healthy creature."

A band starts tightening across the center of my chest. "Well, but why go through all of that if it's not really my own egg? I mean, he —" tipping my head toward Scott, "doesn't even want a baby in the first place. I'm the only reason we're here. If my —

113

contribution — gets cut out — I don't know. It's like all that work — getting me impregnated — and the cost — it's almost like it'd be beside the point." At first, I think I'm disappointed, yet as I say this, I realize I'm hoping for a child, the experience of a family — not necessarily the biology of it. Molecular DNA doesn't really enter into the picture.

Still, the fertility deity looms over me with his long, Nordic face, this bringer of babies, his voice confiding, "You know what this is? You're just afraid of being found out. As long as the parents don't tell, they never have to find out."

Scott says, "Wait, wait — what?"

The doctor's smile cuts to my marrow. "Where they started. Their biological donors."

I sneak a glance at Scott.

The doctor studies my expression, his smile icy. He's a slick of white in his jacket and lemon hair. "Please — don't be prudish. Wait till you see the work I can do! No one would ever suspect, least of all your child. . . ."

I dress quickly, shoulders hunched, gooseflesh in the air-conditioning.

We don't schedule a return visit, leaving behind his office and his chilling voice.

("People do it all the time.") The waiting room flickers behind us, TV monitors beaming ads for egg donors, sperm donors, IVF. An echo chamber, the sounds bouncing off the floors and ceilings. The idea of it — the singular insistence on a biological child, one body, one set of genes, one source — also like an echo chamber.

Gradually, then all at once, this parental resolve begins to overtake me, the decision making itself. I surf the world of children: India, Thailand, China, Kazakhstan — multitudes of orphaned and impoverished kids in every country on earth. I sign up for newsletters and e-mail updates; chat with adoption counselors and foreign adoptees; collect fat packets in the mail — a mountain accumulating on the dining-room table; read blogs and letters, personal accounts from people embarking on journeys they'd never before imagined. Nigeria, Cambodia, Guatemala. It scrambles my sleep, this research; I dream of ice storms. I wake in the dark with an aching jaw, a sense of desolation: This really is a challenge for someone braver, more intrepid, and more organized than I. As I leaf through the materials, my worry mounts. I wake from dark-edged dreams: long corridors in which lights flicker on and off. My hopes shift from country to country — India, Uzbekistan, Nigeria, Romania. So many contradictory labyrinthine rules!

I spend months on research — which stretch into another year — unable to settle on a starting place. There are too many agencies and countries and lawyers. Then, moments of panic: Scott's been right all along — I must not actually want this as much as I'd thought. The process starts to seem like a deliberate test of fortitude. The agency brochures piled in the center of the dining-room table are pushed to one side. For a dinner party, I must clear the table, so I ferry the stacks of folders — their images of radiant faces, tiny hands waving in the air — to the floor of my office; then, days later, scoot them into the corner of our bedroom. They nearly disappear, transforming into makeshift furniture, a place to stack books.

Scott still hasn't agreed to anything, but I notice he no longer sends me links to stories about Americans slowly going bankrupt in Cameroon hotel rooms, awaiting a child. He no longer writes, "There is no way." It seems he doesn't have to. I think he feels sorry for me. I've stopped calling agencies and reading brochures. After two years of discussion and searching, the children shining on the folders seem farther away, as if transmitted from another galaxy. One day, Scott notices I'm using some emptied adoption-agency folders to organize student papers. He hitches an arm around my shoulders. "Maybe . . . ," he says. "Don't give up yet."

CHAPTER FIVE: MOMENT

Five o'clock on a Friday, late in spring, I've been studying adoption materials for at least a million years. The palm trees beyond my office window are stirring with mermaid light, evening coming, drifting in long blue wisps. I'm reading a blog written by two prospective parents who crossed the Russian steppes in a frigid car, searching for a child who may not actually exist. I stand up from the desk, gravitate toward the windows to watch nannies and office workers walking home. Listless, distracted. I can't seem to get the process going. There are fingers of something like despair creeping in around my rib cage. I'm about to admit defeat.

Good excuses are everywhere when you're scared to do something. Pick them like berries off the bushes — too hard; too late; too expensive. Anything but admit it's inside of yourself: you're too scared. I accuse myself of weakness, wonder if that's why I started to write. Because I was too scared to stand up at the table and say it out loud — whatever was hiding in my thoughts. I chose fiction, that protective cloak of imagination, so if anyone I knew ever got angry, I could deny everything, insist *I made it all up.*

Facing the window, I experience a sort of pause. I'm not sure what to call it. Perhaps it's a vision or mirage floated somehow from the gray dwindling light. I imagine setting the table with two round white plates and one small plate decorated with a lamb. I see the plates clearly, though there's nothing like that in our kitchen. Something whispers to me, *Try, try.* A breath in the vertebrae. For a moment, my grandmother Grace, gone more than ten years, is frowning at me from the window's dark glass, just as though she's standing patiently behind me; I see magenta lipstick, pale brows. I blink, look hard at the image, then swivel to face an empty room. An *us'meh,* as Bud would say. Omen. One of destiny's private moments.

All right, Grace. One last call then — a gesture before surrender. The agency materials had tapered off in the mail several months earlier, but I'd received a straggler that day. Already covered by a stack of student papers, the brochure was just a sheaf of stapled pages, a logo of paper-doll cutouts. I slide it out and dial the number on the inside page, certain the office will be closed this late in the day. After the fifth ring, a young voice answers; she asks whether I'm interested in domestic or overseas adoption.

Startled, I hesitate. "Overseas," I blurt. Then add, "I guess."

"You guess." Her voice curves, a hint of humor. "Been researching foreign procedures for a while?"

"Mostly I've been giving up."

"Uh-hunh." She sounds sympathetic but unsurprised. She asks, "Ever considered domestic?"

"Well, but. . . ." No one's suggested this before. I glance at the window. The neighboring houses are now black silhouettes, ink spots. A red bird stands on the bougainvillea outside my window and tweaks its feathers like it wants to be combed. Bird and I stare at each other. "We're weird — as parents go. I don't know how many birth mothers would pick me."

There's a restless bit of silence between us and then the woman begins to explain things to me, her voice calm as a pond. As I listen, I become aware, for the first time in a long while, of feeling myself relax; the space between my ribs increases. There are all kinds of parents, she says, and so many children, right here, all around, who need parents and homes.

"Every adoption is its own thing." Her fine, light voice continues. "Just like every childbirth is different. And each family."

After we hang up, I tip back in my office chair, teetering, considering. Outside, the red bird turns sideways to get a better eyeful. I look back at the phone. It's like discovering the gap in the hedge to a secret garden: Step through the ivy and there it is, the path laid out, one slate stone after another, right in front of your fool self.

Two weeks later, we drive to Sarasota, where a citywide book club is discussing my novel about a woman with foster parents, someone who believed she had been rescued by apes in the rain forest. I'd awakened one day with the character in my head, dictating her story to me. That morning, I was up in bed with a notebook and pen, transcribing, inhabited by her half-lost voice, a kind of misty howl. For months, I felt unlike myself as I wrote, unpersoned and altered by an alien tropical landscape. Before a podium at the public library, I talk about the writing life, confess to the audience that I was raised to consider telling the truth distasteful, even reckless. I tell them the process of becoming a writer has been a long, hard form of private combat — the struggle to become a truth-teller, to find the private places where there is clarity and energy, and to hand it over to readers. I hear murmurs of recognition. A young woman asks if I have children; when I say no, she nods significantly, as though jotting mental notes.

Afterward, Scott and I explore the city streets and eventually come across the big aquarium. It's filled with children running through hallways. They shout at each other and drop candy wrappers and stream around us in twisting currents. Scott raises his eyebrows at me: I pretend not to notice. They shout at the displays of exotic fish and rap on the shark tank. *"Hey, fish!"* Eventually, we come to a quiet spot: windows filled with coral and jellyfish, the space shadowy as a bower. All around, the tanks have slanting lights, the room is dotted with low, bedroomy sounds. The seahorse tank looks dim and satiny and filled with activity. Minuscule creatures bob to and fro in the water, stretching their question-mark bodies and equine profiles; they swoop together, fly apart, filigreed movement.

The exhibit sign says a seahorse is one of the rare creatures in which the male of the species carries developing embryos in a pouch and gives birth. This particular group had recently spawned, the tank alive with seahorse babies, filaments weaving through the water, entwining each other in baroque patterns. We stand together, watching, and the world quiets down. Seahorses. It's liberating in its otherworldly quality, like a promise from another dimension.

Back at the bed-and-breakfast, we open the door and there's a china plate of truffles on the bedspread. Rolled in cocoa powder, the truffles have cunning, pinched-off tops. The inn's proprietor, who'd spent the morning talking to me about food writing, had slipped in afterward. There's also a card: "Welcome to the family!" I hold the plate on my lap and eat three truffles in a row, vaguely bewitched, crossed by a memory of seahorses. Our room is lined with uncovered windows, so it feels as if we're in an enclosed porch, green light bouncing in from the lawn. The room is all-afternoon sunshine, bending green and blue from the waves of the Gulf of Mexico, barely twenty yards from our room. Down to one truffle, plate on my lap, I hear myself saying, "I mean, I can't keep on not-knowing. Are we doing this or not?" I hadn't realized I was going to say it, but then I know I'd had to.

Is he in this moment too, with me?

His hand had curled around mine as we'd watched the seahorses curling together. We'd observed them, silently, for a long time.

The light in the room turns liquid, suspended and pale. And, quietly, he says, "All right."

Chapter Six:
Talking to God

Mother's Day. Creamy cloths on the tables, classical music. Wired with prerevelation nerves, Scott and I sit at the restaurant table: For weeks we've wanted to tell my parents about our plans to adopt, but we've held back. Scott, who frequently has clearer glimpses into my parents than I do, says we'd better make sure we're ready to let go of the far side of the pool. I know what he means. It can be a bad idea to reveal too much to my father: With the slightest inspiration, he will erupt into assumptions and advice. And at this point, we've kept the secret of our deliberations for so long, it's hard to know how to begin. Sometimes it seems as if the story resists its own telling — some silences harden in place, some things so tamped down we forget how to say them. Scott and I talked it over carefully on the drive to Pompano Beach — how we'd open the conversation, how we'd put it, after so many child-free years: Well guys, you're never going to believe this but. . . .

The restaurant itself is scary: There's a server at one's elbow, seemingly at every moment. They fidget over the silverware, snap open napkins and settle them in our laps, refill the water glasses to a hairbreadth of the brims. My husband and I wait for a moment of privacy, looking at each other behind the waiters' backs. We squeeze each other's hands, tap toes under the table, about to begin, when another man in a tuxedo emerges with a tray of cutlery. Eventually, there's a break just after the black jackets clear away our amuse-bouche and before they bring the consommé. But then I start breathing like a landed trout, too anxious to say a word. I wonder if we will just have to raise our child in total secrecy. To my terror and relief, I hear Scott clear his throat lightly and say, "Hey, so we've got some news!"

He looks at me. I manage, "We've decided. . . ." We interlace our fingers. "We're going to adopt a baby."

My parents freeze, spotlit, their silhouettes painted onto the folding curtains behind them. Bud grabs the table, looks from me to Scott back to me again, a big, open-mouthed, not-quite-smile on his face. "You

126

are . . . now, what are you doing?"

"A baby?" Mom puts her hand on Bud's.

"We talked about it and talked about it and we finally decided to go for it," Scott says gently. "We want to start a family."

"Can you believe it?" I ask brightly, trying to penetrate the layers of shocked silence.

A man in a black jacket appears and begins rearranging all the utensils on the table. "The consommé will be arriving at any moment," he informs us.

Bud's hands move to the top of his head, then, very slowly, he lowers his forehead all the way to the tabletop. I've never seen him do that before. The waiter backs away. "Dad? You okay there?"

Mom says quietly, gingerly, "Well, I think. I think it's wonderful. I think a baby is a very, very good thing."

Dad lifts his head a bit, looks from me to Mom back to me again. "I'm happy? I don't know. Am I happy? How do I feel? I can't tell." He slowly returns to an upright position.

Mom faces Dad and says in a fresh, assured way, "It's wonderful. Incredible. A baby — it's a miracle. You're happy, Gus."

Bud looks at her. "I am?" A veil lifts from his features. He turns to me. "But — how — where will you get the baby?"

"Well, Dad, so —"

New ideas glisten in his eyes. "You know what — you can get him from Jordan! Maybe even, can we get a boy baby? I would like that, a boy baby. What will you name him? Maybe you'd like to name him after my father, Saleh. We can all go to Jordan to get him — he might even look like me. I have a cousin who runs an orphanage — she has babies. She can give us a baby."

Mom watches him during this outpouring with a familiar sort of patience. It reminds me of the times when my sisters and I were young girls and Bud would lament, "If we lived in Jordan, you girls would marry royalty. Actual princes." Mom's face would light up and she'd say, "Hey, great, where are the actual princes? Are they coming for dinner?"

Now she says to Bud, "Gus — you aren't the one adopting this baby. Diana and Scott are."

Scott leans forward. "We're going to sign up with an agency in town. It'll be a domestic adoption — I mean, assuming someone picks us."

"Who wouldn't pick you?" Bud's chin is tucked. "I would pick you first."

We've just spent weeks constructing a profile, a kind of life-infomercial, including snapshots of house, car, friends, and family, which the agency gives to birth parents, along with information about your careers, religion, and ethnicity. Scott explains this to my parents, and Bud nods and puts his forearm on the table, taps it. "In Jordan, we don't say we're white or black. We're *qameh.* Which really is the best-looking — you get a little of taste everything. See?" He shows off his tan skin as the waitstaff attempts to exchange one set of bowls with another. *Qameh* means "wheat." "I think the baby should be *qameh,* too. He will be beautiful."

"It doesn't really work so much that way, Dad. They pick us."

"The baby *is* going to be beautiful," Mom tells Bud — now fully embracing the facts. "Whoever this baby is. Whatever she looks like."

The waiters are before us, ladling bowlfuls of steaming brown broth. Plumes of meaty aroma dampen our faces, mesmerizing as incense. Bud leans over his bowl, gazing at a reflection. "Look, there's an *us'meh,*" he breathes. A sign. "The baby will look like me!"

Over the summer, we filled out psychological profiles, got fingerprinted, underwent background checks, submitted a handful of personal recommendations, attended adoption classes, group sessions, parenting workshops. We are settled in for what, by all accounts, will be a good long wait, for a young pregnant woman to point to our pictures and say: Them. It's well into the fall, but the Floridian heat has hung on, a deep, scorching presence with slashes of summer in it. I'm half-writing, my mind in that funny, multilevel pentimento in which thoughts drift over unformed but persistent underthoughts, transparencies of preoccupations, layers superimposed on top of one another. Sometimes I think it would almost be a relief to be pregnant, to let the body take over what's needed and free the mind for a little while longer. But just as with any pregnancy, I'm learning there's a vigilance about adoption — nothing's taken for granted. Every now and then, Scott will stroke my hair, put his lips on top of my head, and say, "How's it going in there?" I'm at my desk, my husband and dog out in the front yard, playing catch. Here is our dailyness, the regular rhythms that bind our days and help keep us as calm as can be managed. Without listening, I hear the sounds of their play, Yogi's regular *woof* at each toss of the ball, Scott's *Go get it!*

Behind all this, the oceanic currents of traffic whirl down the street, just a few doors beyond our house.

There is just a slight pause, a moment that seems tender, like a sag in time. That's what I first notice: not the *woof*, but its absence.

Then a mechanical screech, brakes. Her scream breaking open the wall of my office, a crescendo, higher and louder than any sound she's ever made. Shock enters my body like icy fog. I stand. I can't seem to remember how to walk normally. I tell myself, *okay*.

Scott rushes in the front door as I reach the living room. He says, "She's hit." He says, "Don't go outside."

"Call 911," I gasp, forgetting that Yogi isn't a person.

He wraps his arms around me.

I see, through the open door, our dog's body, a dark pool, a young man in a suit squatting beside her, hands out as if in supplication. The car askew at the side of the road. I stand in the doorway, trying to take it in, but I can't because the world is wavy. There are men working on the roof across the street, yet far away, the neighborhood is silent, the air has turned thin and silvery and hot. My knees and throat feel molten. I cling to the door frame and someone

131

screams at the young man, "YOU KILLED MY DOG." Maybe I didn't scream it. He doesn't seem to hear.

Scott says it happened in a weird, logy, impossible moment — something from the back of a dream. He watched as she turned and casually strolled past our front lawn, right into the street. No reason. The car, he says, materialized.

Scott heads back out, tells the driver, "Go. Get out." The man scuttles to his car, shoulders hunched, and vanishes. We move quickly, before any more cars whirl around the corner. Scott slides her body onto a bit of cardboard and we carry her into the backyard. I place my palm on her side, the silk of her, the ribs as delicate as fish bones; I try to detect the old hum of energy, a steady drum, but she feels flat. Through my shock, I focus on an emerging thought: to bury her myself, to do it with my own hands, in our backyard. We start digging a hole. Then another, and another. Scraping and hacking, here and there and here and there, we discover that our entire yard, and possibly the whole of South Florida, is built on a substratum of coral covered by a few inches of topsoil. We can't carve a hole any deeper than five or six inches. There's a high, white, whining sound in my ears. I tear up our yard while our dog's body grows cold, loosely wrapped in a towel. Finally, Scott brings out bigger tools, chisel, crowbar, and hammer. We don't stop: The harder it is, the harder we push, as though performing some kind of death-duty or penance. We smash away layers of stone, trading the chisel back and forth. Scott can break away twice as much as I can, but I keep swinging and bashing, which is better somehow than crying or praying, sweat streaming down my back, laboring at this small, hard act.

I spend six days outside visiting with our dog in her shallow grave. Each morning, I talk to her and tell her about the day — trying in some way to keep her beside me. I'm squatting by her grave again, knees aching, when I hear the phone ring inside. It's our adoption agency. Our social worker's voice sounds different — shimmering, somehow, almost iridescent. I've never heard her like this. I lower myself slowly into my chair as I hear her saying that there's a pregnant girl — not far away. "Guys — she chose you."

Am I underwater? The air won't come into my lungs. Everything is shiny, ungraspable.

"Are you there? Did you hear me?"

"I can — I am. . . ." I look at Scott, who is staring at me, just inches away, but it's hard to see him clearly, the way tears make everything smeared and waxy.

The social worker faxes the information on record for this woman — her family and medical history: She's single, without work, and six and a half months healthily pregnant. Beyond these bare details, all is mystery.

I put down the pages of medical tests, go outside, and look at the arc of yellow flowers behind our house, blossoms curling into tiny bubbles. For the past week, I've been subsisting on sips of broth, tea, crackers, not a trace of sugar: a grief diet. I climbed out of bed and the clang of sadness sent me straight back. "Someone is coming," I murmur to the ground. "You knew." This might be the closest I've come to prayer in years. As I rise from my crouch beside her grave, the palm trees lift their fronds, sailing on the midwinter air.

A few weeks after we learn we've been "matched," a social worker calls to ask if we'd like to meet the woman who will give birth to our daughter. Our birth mother, she's called, as if she will be delivering all of us.

I spend days thinking about gifts. Nothing is right. In despair, I settle on a basket to fill with fruit, cheeses, nuts, and chocolates. We pile up the big woven basket. It occurs to me this will also be a gift to our child. I try to find the sweetest Satsuma oranges, the rosiest pomegranate. I imagine whispering to the baby: Have a taste of this and this — cashews and macadamias and strawberries dipped in chocolate, buttery shortbreads scented with vanilla, triangles of Camembert and winey grapes. On the day of our meeting, I change clothes until my hair's crackling with static, everything in a floor heap. My nerves are hectic, sprung, my breath feels raw. I glare at my reflection: Does this make me look like a mother? Does this?

The drive isn't long, but it feels Odyssean. The sky stretches into elastic blueness and white, architectural clouds. The birth mother's social worker decided we'd meet at an Olive Garden. Bud hooted, "In an olive garden! Jordan is all olive gardens! And lemon trees. It's an *us'meh.*" That's how the *us'meh* is: dreadful or funny or miraculous, and always unquestionable. We pull into a vast parking lot, a shopping-mall sea. I picture decades of jangled adoptive families gathering here to wonder, meet, pace, and fret. Scott and I have arrived too early and wait in the front window-lined lobby, holding hands tightly. I gaze with beagle eyes at everyone who pushes through the doors. At two o'clock on a Sunday afternoon, every woman walking into the Olive Garden is seven months pregnant. The room seems slightly tilted, noises zoom around us, in and out of focus. I pat the hair out of my eyes over and over, my hands damp.

Scott's eyes lift over my head, to the parking lot beyond, and stay there. Then I turn too.

That's her. We just know. She has brave, erect shoulders and her eyes are lowered. I feel abashed, suddenly uncertain; twelve years old in the middle-school gym, eyeing my square-dance partner. I watch through the glass as she approaches, an echo bounces between us like déjà vu. We are versions of each other — tall and angular, our faces have the same flat planes. Crazy hair. The glass door flashes, she walks in, bringing a bolt of humid air from outside. Somewhere in the distance, a lawn mower growls awake. Connie, the social worker, introduces us to Lilah and her boyfriend. She signals us from behind Lilah, shakes her head, rolls her eyes, mouths: NOT THE DAD.

I take Lilah's hand; soft as a wish. This is all so almost-normal. We're seated in a quiet, open area to the right, at a big round table. The social worker places herself like a plump hen between me and the young woman. "Can you believe the traffic? It's crazy — they're like crazy people!" Connie swabs her forehead with a folded napkin. "Every time I come out to this mall I think, that's *it* — I'm giving up on shopping. It's not for me. Sometimes I wonder if I'm cut out to be an American — you know? Like maybe I should go try Portugal or Sweden or someplace. Because really, what's the point anyway? All of this rush, rush, rush. Where they all rushing to?" She rattles on, her small head turning from me to Lilah to me to Lilah.

Scott tries to lean around her and address Lilah. "We were so glad you wanted to meet. It's not every day that —"

"Oh, no, it isn't, is it?" Connie intercepts him. "None of us hardly go to this side of town. And now it's getting toward the holidays — well, forget it. It's not going to get better." She scolds as if he'd asked her to direct traffic.

Lilah holds her menu up like a mantilla, shyly covering her face. When the waiter comes, she and Miguel stare at him, blinking and speechless. Connie orders antipasto for the table. "Please — whatever you like,"

Scott urges them. "Take it home if you don't finish."

Lilah orders in a nearly transparent voice. Twice, the waiter asks her to repeat herself. Once he leaves, Connie resettles herself, smooths out her skirt, and begins quizzing Lilah: Where did she grow up? What did her parents do? How did she get her hair like that? She fingers a lock of Lilah's hair as if this were a perfectly normal thing to do. "So you use a curling iron or is it like that naturally?"

"I straight-iron then curl it." Lilah looks bemused. "Why you asking so much about my hair?"

Connie sniffs, rests her chin on the back of her curled fingers, and turns toward the window. I hold a section of my own hair. "This drove my parents crazy. Dad was always saying . . ." — I switch to a Jordanian accent — " 'Make there less of it!' "

Lilah lets go of a wisp of laughter, then glances at Miguel. "My mother don't like my nails," she allows, flaring out her fingers. A tattoo of musical notation spirals up her arm. Connie leans between us. "Diana is a *college professor,*" she murmurs in a low voice, as if to say professors don't approve of nail polish.

Lilah sinks into her seat, edging toward

Miguel, who hasn't stopped smirking. Scott nudges my foot under the table. He asks Lilah, "Did you like being in school?"

A look at Miguel. "Sure."

I try, "Did you have any favorite classes?"

A shrug, her lids like hoods, hiding places; her face is crossed with shadows. "I don't know. . . ."

"Oh, now I loved social studies." Connie begins tearing a slice of bread into pieces. "I thought I'd become a teacher. Maybe I missed my calling? Who honestly knows? Okay, but now my fifth-grade homeroom teacher. . . ." She prattles on, buttering each of the little bits. I imagine pushing her under the table.

Lilah's gaze flits to mine. Her eyes tip and her lips wrinkle slightly, as if she's thinking about laughing.

So, dessert. Connie picks something for the table that turns out to be a big block of chocolate covered in whipped cream, scrolled with chocolate sauce and tiled with chocolate curls like wood shavings. Lilah and Miguel lean forward, hands on their laps. Connie wedges a fork in one corner and gets stuck. Lilah and Miguel wait for her to work out the one bite, then they go at it, cutting in, closing their eyes as they eat. Scott speaks to a waiter, and when the man returns with our check, he hands Lilah a takeout box containing another brick of chocolate.

I hang back to walk out with her. She lowers her head, slides hands in her pockets. I ask if she's tired. She says, "Oh, yes, I am. Can't wait to get my jeans back on." Her sugar-drunk smile lingers. "The normal ones."

Connie says, "How about a picture?" We stand in the lot beside the dusty backs of cars. Between Scott and Lilah, I put an arm around each of them. In the shot, I'm grinning, chin tucked, goofy, unbalanced; Scott is more reserved with the weight of the moment, and Lilah gazes into another direction, her smile quiet and private, her eyes sleepy, as if, with a little more sun and a spot of grass, she could curl up for a nap. The hidden one is also there, of course, asleep beneath our arms, full of pasta, cream sauce, and chocolate.

Strange, to know one is predestined, appointed, to fall in love before meeting the beloved; like the presage of bouquet before the wine. It seems that pregnancy isn't limited to the physical but fills the mind, colors the soul. She is coming, the air whispers; she is somewhere.

Seven weeks later, the highway swims before our eyes, its path blurring and shifting in the predawn. I keep seeing imps in the roadside shrubbery. Scott didn't get any more sleep than I did, but he drives easily, eyes soft, resembling someone who feels calm and clear-headed. Lilah has scheduled a birth induction today. At 4:00 a.m., Scott and I sat up in bed, looked at each other, the suitcases waiting like ghosts in the gloom, and he said, "Okay?"

"Yeah."

"Let's go."

Halfway into the three-hour drive, my cell phone rings; it's the birth mother's social worker, Connie. "Um, don't leave quite yet."

I'm holding the phone tightly; calls from Connie have this effect on me. "What do you mean? We left! We left hours ago. We want to be there for the birth."

There's a reshuffling sort of pause. Finally, she says, "Well, the thing is, they're trying to talk her out of it."

Scott is trying to drive and watch me at the same time. I turn toward my side window. "Who is trying to talk who —"

"It's a thing these days. . . ." She releases an aggravated breath. "These religious types get a hold of the nurses and start trying to tell them religious things. Evangelicals or something. Are they all over the place down there? They think that kids should only be raised by their birth mothers. No other choices. Nobody else ever."

The agency brochures didn't mention this. I hunch into the phone, tucking my elbows on my knees. "Aren't fundamentalists, like, antiabortion?"

"Who knows? They just want to dictate the whole deal — no abortions and no adoptions, no nothing. They think it's all just gonna be handy-dandy. Birth mothers don't have any say in any of it, as far as they're concerned. It's the people on the bottom that always get sat on."

"But Connie?" I hunch closer to the phone. "Do we stop? What are we doing now?"

"No, no, no. You're already this far. Come on."

Connie assures me, before hanging up, "Lilah's been clear from the get-go, this is what she wants. There's just — you know — some idiots and maniacs trying to freak her out."

I don't remember saying goodbye. I sit holding the cell, gazing ahead, sleepiness a dull weight at the back of my head.

■ ■ ■ ■

We pull into the familiar circular driveway:
My in-laws' house is just half an hour from
our birth mother's hospital. We'll stay with
them as we wait for the baby. Geraniums
and loquats and oranges are blooming in
their yard. When I first met my father-in-
law, Dave walked around the front yard with
me, plucking ripe fruit; we inhaled its
incense. He and I filled a paper bag with loquats from the tree in the front yard. Six
feet six, he was able to reach the fruit on
the highest branches. He kept asking questions; it was our first meeting, and Dave
was incorrigibly curious: "When do you
write?" "What does your last name mean?"
"What do you think of Yasir Arafat?" "Did
you grow up with pets?" "How do you say
'loquat' in Arabic?"

There's no fruit my own father loved more
than the loquat: tiny, tender plums, rare and
sweet. For thirty years, Dave had more or
less ignored them as they bloomed and
burst on his front lawn. When Scott and I
took my parents a grocery bag filled to the
brim with Dave's fruit, Bud stared, lifted
one with reverence. "This, look. This is *es-
kidinia.*"

143

The first time my father and my father-in-law met, Bud arrived with peaches and wine-dark grapes he'd bought from a man selling them from a truck tire on the side of the road. "Dave, Dave!" Bud nearly jumped out of the car, leaving Mom to collect their bags. "You have to try these guys. You'll love these guys."

I hadn't introduced them yet. Bud held a bunch, but Dave's hands were filled with tools or potting soil. He leaned forward to see and my father put a grape in his mouth.

Dave took a step back. Then he said, "That is good." After a pause, he added, "I don't think I've ever been fed by a man before." For years, the memory returned to him at random moments and he would tell the story again.

Dave still lives at the lakeside home where his children grew up. The kids got married and moved away, Dave divorced, remarried, but stayed at the old place. The yard rambles down to the water, filled with fish, gators, egrets. A few miles away rise the steaming freeways of Orlando, a dreary downtown, but here you can smell tangerine, avocado, acres of citrus fields, the freshness from the lake washing the air. And there is Dave, tall and good-looking, affable as Jimmy Stewart, reaching the highest branches or bent over his workbench, tinkering.

Just a few months ago, he was diagnosed with lung cancer, though he'd never touched a cigarette. Now he's on oxygen: still genial, but propped in bed. Within a month, the medications have distorted his body — shrinking and then bloating him. He's no longer hungry; his wife Judie struggles to find something that tempts him. We bring him crackers that are made out of nuts — mostly for the novelty — anything at the market that looks interesting or distracting. One of his lungs is filling with the hard, gnarled substance of tumor: It's overtaking him, despite radiation and caustic treatments, tearing at him the way a dropped stitch unravels a whole sweater. We talk about guided imagery, tai chi, acupuncture, massage therapy. He is open to all sorts of alternative therapies. As his body breaks down, his mind seems to be growing freer and wilder. People keep calling and dropping by, bringing food, offering services. Dave and Judie curl up in their airy bedroom, watching TV, the rafters of leaves beyond their windows.

Scott and I drop our bags then pace between the rooms, waiting to hear something, scanning the heaps of food Dave's friends have dropped off — piles of coffee cakes, Danish, boxed doughnuts. The phone rings at 7:00 a.m.: "They started inducing a while ago," Connie says. "I forgot to mention that. But don't come to the hospital."

7:40: "She definitely wants this adoption, there's no question. She says you can come soon."

8:14: "That nurse just doesn't want her to do it. She thinks she can get Lilah a job at Burger King."

8:50: "Okay, well — she doesn't want you at the birth."

Ah, disappointment. I feel a pressure between my ribs, flat and aching, like swallowed tears. "No. Of course. We understand. Can we come right after?"

"Sure. Probably."

Around 10:30, the four of us assemble for breakfast, the counter stacked with donated bakery boxes, a drift of icing, cheese filling, toasted pecans, apple strudel, apricot glaze. Between the wheeze and thump of the oxygen machine and the jingling phone, we lean on our elbows and chat with Dave and Judie about parenting.

"Don't let the kid know you're a socialist," Dave warns me.

"I promise, I won't."

"What are you going to tell her about the

war on terror?"

Judie rolls her eyes and balls up her napkin. "Here we go."

"I'll probably wait till she's three or four to get into that."

He laughs, then says, "No, but really?"

Scott says, "Yeah, she might want to know sooner. Her first words might be *threat level orange.*"

Dave laughs, then scowls. "I'm glad you think terror is funny."

Judie says, "For Pete's sake, David."

"But just for the sake of argument — like when she asks about President Bush —"

"Which she will," Scott says. "Obviously."

"*If* she asks about Bush — how are you going to describe him?"

I hunch and hold up claws. "He was squinty and he laughed like 'heh, heh, heh.'"

The phone spins and whirs: We jump. Scott takes it into the next room. Each call has gotten progressively more nerve-wracking, so we've taken to trading back and forth. I can hear his voice lift, he runs back to the table. "Gracie's born! She's healthy, almost eight pounds!"

"Oh." It's a rush like a bucket of water over the head; my shoulder blades seem to unpin, my chest fills. "Oh my God."

Judie hugs us. Dave drums the table, then stops to catch his breath. "But how long is she?"

Scott nods, phone pressed against his ear. "She's as long as an otter! But apparently she's already registered with the socialist party."

Dave's smile is brief and sneaky. "Joke now. That's right. Just wait."

I'm clutching the table. "Can we go see her?"

Scott snaps the phone shut. "She says in an hour. She'll call soon."

We call people, crowing, "Eight pounds! Sea otter!" Mostly we wander around aimlessly from room to room, until Judie asks us to take it outside. We hold hands and stroll through the lakeside neighborhood, wild-eyed sleepwalkers. We check the cell every twenty minutes, but an hour passes, then two. Three. Waiting to see our daughter, to hear news, gradually becomes a form of low-grade torment. I note an incipient ache in my throat like a knot, my breath pushed to the top of my lungs. The swimming gestures of the palm trees, the crenellated surface of the gray lake, the silent, matter-of-fact cars and bikes and dogs and billboards — everything is otherworldly and heartlessly normal, as if this could be just another day. By two o'clock, I beg Scott to call Connie. Vagabonds, we sit on the grass in front of his father's house. Scott hunches over into the phone. "Hey, it's us again." Long pause. "Scott and Diana?" Pause. "Okay. Okay. Okay. Is it — look, is she changing her mind or anything? Yes, but, I see, okay. Is she going to change her mind?" He's up and doing a boardroom pace, back and forth, over the front lawn. "So — okay. Okay. Okay." He closes the phone and looks at me: I can practically see him trying to order his thoughts.

"She changed her mind," I say quietly. "She doesn't want to do it."

"No, no," Scott's voice is light and crisp. "Not exactly. I don't know." He lowers himself to the grass, puts an arm around my shoulders. "I guess she's just not totally sure she wants us to come to the hospital today. I mean, right this second."

Thoughts run in pieces through my fingers. Over these days and months, I've formed an attachment, a link — invisible and intangible, yet very real — to our growing child who-is-not-yet-our-child. Yet I must, it seems, be prepared to relinquish her, to do it with good grace and equanimity. "We don't have to bother her — we won't go by her room. If we could just stop by the nursery and peep at the baby? We don't even have to hold her — just, you know, to see her."

Scott takes my hand and there's something in the gentleness of this gesture that makes the skin prickle up the back of my neck. I know I should feel lucky for the love in my life, yet already I'm hungry for this one as well.

"She doesn't want us to go into the hospital. She doesn't want us in the building."

"Did she say that? The building? Did the social worker tell you that?"

Lilah and Connie have turned into "she" and "the social worker."

"She made it pretty clear. 'She wants to take a nap and rest and she doesn't want to think about anything.' She says she can't relax if we're in the building."

"Oh." My head lowers. "God, I'm no good at this." I feel spinning anxiety that she is about to change her mind. What chutzpah, it occurs to me now, that I'd never even considered this possibility before. The agency had mentioned that birth mothers will change course about a quarter of the time — generally, not surprisingly, right after giving birth. That percentage had wisped past me like smoke signals. Later, a

150

social worker will confide it's closer to half and half.

Now Scott pulls me in so I can feel the scruff of his grown-out shave on top of my head. "Hang on," he says. I feel the sigh fill and exit his chest.

We'd thought we'd be at this birth and hold our daughter in her first hours. A dry little swallow, tight throat, my broody self; caught in the usual spaces between expectations and reality. I feel a bump of guilt over how angry I used to get with Gram and her talk of disappointment. Our relationship became more layered and complicated when I entered my teens and began to notice how I'd been unwittingly enlisted in her war with Bud. "Stop telling me those stories," I'd barked at her once. "All that about horrible men. I don't hate men — I'm not like you!" She was hurt and amazed. "I don't hate men, either," she'd said. "I'm just telling you how it is."

Now it seems she'd wanted to warn me, to brace me for whatever we couldn't know, couldn't even guess was coming. But when you haven't yet felt big disappointment, such talk can feel like someone is trying to rob you of happiness, darkening the colors. Grace just wanted me to be ready.

■ ■ ■ ■

Winter Park, an upscale suburb, is a place where life appears to take a little less effort. Pregnant mothers are draped in linens, their babies transported in cloudlike beds, on wheels that scarcely touch the ground. No one cries on these sidewalks. Trying to distract ourselves, we stroll, peer through windows at twinkling pendant lamps and low, creamy couches. While we're sitting at a café, not touching our food, the phone rings. I seize it, then close my eyes. "Hi."

"Tonight at the very latest!" Connie's voice bounces. I imagine a rubber ball going up and down. It keeps moving, just out of range.

That evening, we sit with Dave watching the news. Tomorrow is the presidential inauguration of Barack Obama. Dave shakes his head, smiling. "The things you never thought you'd ever see." He and his wife sit crooked together on the big recliner. They had planned to finally take a trip to Europe this summer. Judie canceled the tickets a few days ago. At the back of their house is a terrace with vines and a trellis and many windows and doors that the summery night glides through. It carries the sound of field

152

insects, a familiar scent of hot earth and roads. We watch more news then switch to World War II documentaries. But my attention keeps wandering to the night shining in the doors, the silent telephone on the kitchen counter, 8, 9, 10 o'clock and no call. Finally, at 11 o'clock, Scott's cell rings. He leaves the room. I don't have the heart to follow. I've been trying to coach myself to accept reversal, to look at it all dispassionately, with curiosity, the way that Dave, with his engineer's mind, tells the pulmonary technicians midprocedure that he finds getting his lung drained "fascinating." Dave has had long talks with Scott in which he confesses to great curiosity about this whole business of illness and dying. "I keep wondering if I'm going to have some big emotional reaction. But so far, not so much, really. . . ."

Why can't I do that? Pull back a little? We haven't once held this baby or looked into her eyes, but I am bereft at the thought of losing her. Scott has reassured me that if Lilah changes her mind we'll just wait for the next baby. "Remember what Bud says about *us'meh*? We can't fight this stuff." His gaze is steady. "We'll have the baby we're meant to have."

Yes, okay. Then I think, *no.* This baby. I

153

feel it all the way to the small bones in my fingers.

Scott returns to the room; we look at him. He gestures for me to come back in the bedroom. I sit with him and say again, "She's changed her mind. It's okay."

He shakes his head. "Connie says she still wants to do it. But we can't see the baby yet. Lilah wants to be left alone tonight."

He holds the side of my head. I hold his arm. We sit together like that, very still, not talking, just waiting.

Hi Buddies,

Hooray!! Grace (Coquina? Nalani? Anaya? Bimini?) Abujaber-Eason was born today, 7 pounds 11 ounces, without very much hair. Dad asked if she looks like me, to which we say, yes, she looks exactly like both of us.

Just one little detail, we haven't actually met her yet. . . . It may be another day or so before we can swoop in and actually stare at our little bean. If anyone has any advice on how to achieve deep Zen states of patience, please let us know.

Xxx

D and S

We wake before dawn, peering at each other's outlines in the shadow. Gray light tilts into the room, filtering through the windows, rising slowly, faintly, a flinty shadow softening to pearl, a nearly invisible blue sky, the transparency of skin. On the kitchen counters, there's another big breakfast: more well-wishers have come with doughnuts, cakes, fruits, cellophane boxes for my in-laws. So many plates, bags, and boxes stacked, toppling across the counter. We nibble pastry without much appetite, and eventually drift back into the TV room. The screen flashes with images of Obama's inauguration. Together, we watch the assemblies of new political figures, a procession through the building, emerging to the doors, press, and crowds. Obama's family is there, the previous administration as well, the smirking, outgoing president: Such a sharp contrast between the last of the good old boys and whatever this new paradigm will be. On his ceremonial walk to the people, Obama moves fluidly. He has a fine, upright head, an open bearing; he scans the sky, the Capitol grounds, collected, waiting. The massive crowd can't stop cheering — wave after wave crests. The churning crowds, ceaseless shattering applause, the ecstatic sense of a future radiates from the screen. Several times during the broadcast my breath catches; tears slide down my face. The world is so immense at this moment, filled, it seems, with revelations. Even my father-in-law is moved. He shakes his head. "You know? I voted for the other one, but I can't help feeling excited. Funny. Like, you just really want the guy to do good."

The phone rings. I can't hear Connie over the cheering on the TV, so I ask her to wait. Once I'm sitting alone in the front yard, I say, "Okay?"

She says, "Get ready!"

I'm a little disoriented, my emotions radiant and blurred: I don't know whether my eyes are damp from the TV, from the phone call, from the way the light sharpens and vibrates on the orange tree leaves. "Today?" I stand up. "Really, you're sure?"

"You'll take your daughter home."

First: delays. Lilah doesn't want to wait in the hospital to complete the adoption paperwork. She's ready to clear out, so the social worker, the agency's lawyer, a notary, and two witnesses need to be reassembled at Lilah's home before anything can happen. "Can we call anyone for you?" I tug on an orange leaf, its fragrance rising out of leftover rain. "Drive someone somewhere?

Anything?"

Just dig down and wait, Connie advises, they're working on it.

Odd reports come in, scattering around us, bits of confetti in the air: One of the birth mother's friends thinks the baby is too pretty to give up and maybe the friend wants to keep her. The birth mother thinks of a few other men who might be the father, potentially requiring us to formally notify several more people of this birth. The evangelical nurse feels that she needs to have another sit-down with Lilah. The birth mother decides that we should get to the hospital within the next ten minutes to prove our dedication. Connie calls back minutes later: No, wait. The day stretches out. The phone's ring hardens, a small, cranial hammer. Each previous snarl melts away before the new one. Scott tries to console me, saying at least we're not doing this in a frozen Eastern-bloc country, pockets filled with baksheesh. Then he pauses, adding, Well, maybe today is a compressed version of the freezing Eastern-bloc-country experience. I send a series of e-mail updates to my sisters and a few friends; they counsel patience and calm distance: "Unfocus your eyes," someone writes. My friend Lola suggests a nap. This strikes me as almost comical — as if anyone could relax! I stretch out in the guest bedroom with a thought of attempting to meditate and free-fall into sleep.

An hour later, there's the sound of a voice through the wall. Scott is talking on the cell in the hallway. The door eases open; for a moment, I see just his eyes. The door creaks as he enters, a small, quiet smile on his face, and I feel all the blood in my body begin to levitate; breath leaves me. He says, "Time to meet her."

The short winter day is already arcing toward its close. On the highway, I see shreds of unexpected color in the sky, the clouds high and massing like their own mysterious country, backlit and ineffable. But the traffic! The drivers race after each other's taillights on the rainy highway, throwing out spume. At one bend, we watch in the rearview mirrors two swerving cars collide just behind us like bumper cars, then spin off to either side of the road. We just keep going.

Once we finally get there, it takes far too long to find the entrance to the hospital complex, too long to find parking, too long to run to the front door, for someone to direct us, in our adrenalized, headlight-dazed state, to the right lobby. We have to stand still and smile for photos, placed in ID badges looped over our heads, in order to be allowed to enter. Before sending us upstairs, the security guard with a short, gray nimbus of curls stops us to squeeze our arms. He rumbles, "God bless you two."

The corridor leading to the nursery has closed-circuit monitors and a steel double door that unlocks with a mechanical thump, like something in a medium-security prison. We speak our names into the intercom and the door vibrates, whirs open. Scott takes my hand: It's like walking onstage, only this stage is hushed and crowded with tiny, even breaths and bassinets propped here and there on wheeled carts. The big room is shadowy, translucent with sleep. A nurse holding a clipboard looks up, smiling broadly — to my relief. She says, "Scott and Diana?"

We stand still, surrounded by this galaxy of dreaming babies. I breathe, "Which one?"

She lifts her chin.

My arm is touching the bassinet. She's wearing one of their little knit caps, jaunty as an elf, her slate-gray eyes partially open, glimmering in a half-state, watching, just as though she's been expecting us.

They wheel the bassinet into a private room. When the nurse lifts the drowsy, soft bundle into my arms, a sob breaks from my throat, my eyes flood with tears. The nurse turns away as she leaves the room. Scott's eyes are dark and wet as he touches her head. I don't know how to hold a baby. My hands feel big and clumsy; we're so new to each other. Her diaphanous fingers open and close carefully about my thumb. We feed her a minute bottle, then later, at the nurse's coaxing, dare to change her diaper, her limbs rubbery, bent into froggy folds. Her paper ears lie flat against her head, intricate as origami. She is the color of my palm, soft as a blush, a song.

After a couple more hours of paperwork, notaries, interviews, and observation, the door to the nursery opens. I am, as first mothers go, unsteady. Wiping off her tiny body in the nursery sink, we're terrified of spilling water over her head, anxious to get the swaddling right. I need to stop in the ladies' room before we leave, but I hesitate: Can I just "dash" into the bathroom? Do I take the baby? Do I hold her? Where do I put her? Thankfully, the nursery attendant kindly offers to watch our child. I stare at the inside of the restroom stall door, staggered by how little I know.

It's a frosty day for Florida, a thin January

wind curls through the air. I cover the bassinet with blankets, curve my body around the sleeping inhabitant as I carry her, dismayed to have to take this small being out into the cold. We move quickly, clipping her into the car seat. The nursery attendant and the social worker stand shoulder to shoulder in the hospital entrance like Bogart and Rains. "Congratulations!" They wave at us. "You'll be great! Don't be scared — it's only a baby!"

As promised by friends with kids, she sleeps through the four-hour ride. Scott drives, I sit in the backseat holding her silky hand, marveling. I say at least once, in complete astonishment, "There's a baby in our car."

When we get home, we walk in and set her, still dozing in her bassinet, right on top of the dining-room table. We sit at the table beside her, holding hands, breathing lightly, watching her sleep. The air feels curved and sparkly, as though we were seated inside a soap bubble. We hold each other's gaze a moment. This is our first prayer, this wordless pause. A plea for blessings, addressed to all the unknown places, the darkness between the stars, the machinery of dreams. My synapses feel electrified, racing up and

down my spine with raw fear and elation.
Our child. Our Gracie.

■ ■ ■ ■

PART III
GOOD EATER

■ ■ ■ ■

CHAPTER SEVEN:
EASY

When a child is born into a family, someone new enters the room. Who, pray tell, is this? one asks. And deeper, beneath that question lies another: Now who am I? Am I still the same?

When Bud wasn't searching for houses, he frequently looked for a son. Not having that little boy seemed to make him feel less than himself. As if our family wasn't quite yet our family. When I was twelve, Suzy eight, Monica seven, our father solemnly sat us at the bargaining table. He and Mom had talked things over, he said — our eyes skated to our mother — and they wanted to know how we'd feel about adopting a baby. In theory. There wasn't an *actual* baby, of course, just the idea of one. But a boy, to be specific. He wanted to adopt a son.

Shock percolated among us, the air bubbled. There were too many questions: Really? How soon? Where would he come from? How would we get him? There were also all sorts of questions that we kept to ourselves, such as: Do you want a child or a boy? And, if your first child had been a boy, does that mean there would have been fewer daughters? None of us?

We'd grown up hearing Dad's relatives call him "Abu Jaffer." Arabs are referenced by their children. "Abu" means father of, and this title is commonly followed by the name of the firstborn son. Long ago, in a reckless moment, Dad apparently had bragged that he would produce a handsome, hearty son and this boy would be named Jaffer. Why Jaffer? "It means 'lovely stream,' " Bud explained with his usual opacity. Ever after, he was tormented by this nickname, Abu Jaffer, mocking his absent heir, his track record of only daughters. "He's ABU DIANA," I used to roar at these uncles and cousins in their slacks and sideburns, cracking them up. Bud never backed me up, though, instead busying himself with turning the kabobs on the grill, burning his fingers, never a pot holder. "Abu Jaffer!" they yelled at him. "When's dinner ready?"

Around the curved sectional couch my sisters, parents, and I sat, the circular glass coffee table before us, the steel arc of the

166

floor lamp above, waiting for someone to stand too quickly and smack their head. Bud hunched forward, elbows on his knees, his eyes so soft and ardent they looked candlelit: He explained how this was his heart's desire, the missing piece — if only we could all help fill it in.

"Or?" he added. "We could get a swimming pool."

All eyes skidded back to Mom. She lifted her eyebrows at us.

Bud sighed. "That's our other idea here. We saved just enough so we could get a baby — or, right, we could get a pool. You know — put it over in the side yard? We can't afford both — but one maybe we could." He sat straighter, looking each of us in the eye, his tunneling gaze. "So we talked it over, you know, and we think — your Mom and me — *you* girls should decide."

Who knows why? They'd never asked for our input before — not on any of our house moves or how to spend our summers or even what we'd have for dinner. Maybe it was some sort of test of strength or character. Maybe he really thought we'd have a different answer. Maybe he knew somehow, grasped some wisp of self-awareness, of his own powerful ambivalence. It was possible Bud was already figuring out that he didn't know what he wanted or needed to be happy. He only knew that he wanted, not what it was.

My sisters and I repaired to the kitchen for a private session. At the Formica table with the sparkling chips, we gaped at each other and said things like, "Now what?" This was the first any of us had heard of a baby boy. We'd been in this house for a year and I was already holding my breath, dreading the reappearance of the For Sale sign on the front lawn, the inevitable next move to parts unknown. Filled with gravitas, I settled my fingers along the table's edge, inhaled, then looked at my sisters. "Here's what I think. No regular human can figure out this kind of question. So! I think: If the phone rings in the next sixty seconds, then it's a sign to us. From, like, heaven."

"Like a stop sign?" Monica asked.

"Right. It's a sign of *something*." I put my fingers to my temples and closed my eyes. In addition to discovering black-light posters, I'd recently started reading about ESP and the occult. "If the phone rings, then we should get the baby. Definitely. That means we have to do it."

Suzy asked, "Well, what if the phone doesn't ring?"

I opened my eyes and smiled. We stared at

the second hand on the wall clock. After sixty quiet seconds, we ran out to give them the good news.

Bud never adopted his baby, but he went through life gathering others to him, attracting this one and that, cottoning to strangers for no good reason. He invited people over because he liked the rake of a grin or the flower in a buttonhole. Because someone stood beside him at a street corner, waiting for the same light to change. So many invitations to dinner. He left family back in another country and began finding more people nearly everywhere.

I learned from him: No telling where family comes from. It's something richer than blood. It can be made and unmade and made again. It waits patiently to be claimed, taken indoors, for another place to be set at the table. The Qur'an says, *We are one human family, make peace with your brothers and sisters.* Another way of saying, I think, put out more plates. I've felt the sense of kinship inside dinner clubs and writing groups and classes — sometimes strong and whole, other times just hints, tendrils twining around your legs, the way grass seems to grow up around your fingers and toes if you sit in a spot long enough, the earth table. Family is all around, calling your name in the mornings, asking you to listen. Here we are, and you, you're already home.

Her head is like a grapefruit my father cups in the palm of his hand, her swaddled form draped in his lap. They gaze at each other. Bud makes an O with his lips; we watch Gracie's mouth go round, a pop of surprise: There you are! "I knew it was you," he crows softly. "How did I know it was you?" He insists they've known each other "from way back," though she is eight days old. "Her and me," he croons. He chants an annoying old rhyme:

Sabahlkhair, ya ghazal ibbrair!
kul ahlick shin'n, inti helwa mnain?
inti jeeti zeyyithum!

Roughly and unrhymingly translated:

Good morning, oh gazelle of the desert
Your whole family is ugly, so where are you from?
You came to them to make them beautiful!

He carries her through the neighborhood, through shopping malls, through car dealerships, with his inexplicable brag, "I knew it was her!" He kisses her head and ears and tells us she has his nose, and she looks up at us with her wise eyes. "This is my baby."

She studies him so sternly when he gives her a bottle that he laughs with nerves. She softens in his arms, a bleb of ice cream in a blanket. He urges us to go out, enjoy ourselves, makes a shooing motion with his free hand. Mom decides to run a few errands. My husband and I stroll through St. Augustine, where my parents recently moved. We hold hands, notice each other's faces, recall each other's arms. But the call comes in half an hour: She is crying so loudly the tears take on a sheen through the cell phone, a metallic whang. At first it's all I can hear, then somewhere in the background, John the Baptist in a wilderness of crying, there is Bud calling, panic-stricken, "She is awake! I don't know why! What's wrong! Come back. Hurry, hurry."

We fly, driving too quickly, jumping out of the car in the driveway like actors in a cop show, both of us a blur of fear and self-reproach. My seventy-two-year-old father is out of practice with babies — what were we thinking? The door swings open; it's so still inside that a shudder runs through me, a golden sliver through the heart. In the living room we find Gracie pillowed on her grandfather's stomach, the two of them placidly watching Al Jazeera while Bud eats sliced cucumbers. "What? Look. All settled. We're fine. We understand each other." He makes a calm-down-already flap with his hand. "Why you came rushing? It was nothing. Everything is easy."

An easy baby. The creature parents fantasize and whisper about. We take her on jaunts: for her checkup, a stroll through the park. She dozes in her carriage. Passing strangers and older children peep in at her, delighted. She stirs for short visits, barely waking, her mild features agog at the world. Her eyes don't quite obey each other yet, slipping lazily out of alignment from time to time; she frowns, her swimmer's hands reaching out at this hazy world. Mornings, we lay her in a patch of sunlight like a houseplant, to warm away jaundice; she drowses and stretches.

She is our beautiful mystery, a storybook placed on our laps. Open it to the first page and it's written backward and forward, dream-language. Each day we expect a repeat of yesterday, but every day is different. We have a dawning awareness of a parent's new self that had, prior to children, lain dormant within, beside all the other selves — daughter, say, or wife, or baker.

This is a germination, this seed splitting itself open, revealing a fresh, fiercer love and possessiveness. Who are you? I ask the reflections I catch in car windows and storefronts. My child stretches across my chest, clinging; if someone takes her, she cries out, her face caves: I don't relax until I have her back.

Then, life accelerates. At all hours there's the sound of a roiling boil in the kitchen. Scott stands over a cauldron, sterilizing glass bottles. Every minute of every day, we seem to be moving between boiling pieces, assembling bottles, warming formula, feeding baby, sterilizing the bottles. Barely time to eat or sleep. Scott comes back from the store with bags heaped with Pop-Tarts and beer. Fine, I think. I shrug off notions of nutrition. Mom comes on the fifth day. She scoops Gracie up, whispering to her, murmuring, bouncing, walking, and our baby nestles into her. At night, the three adults rotate among the couch, an air mattress on the nursery floor, and our bedroom — the only real bed in the house. Repeatedly, it's 3:00 a.m., one person is up cradling Gracie, feeding her as she fusses, and the other two are also up, staring like statues, addled by sleeplessness.

On the eighth day, Mom calls Bud. She

tells him to come and to "bring food." She says, "Hurry."

Bud arrives from St. Augustine with loaves of pita, chopped salad, and a kettle of stacked, stuffed grape leaves. I take the pots and put Gracie into his arms. At first he's wordless, fish-mouthed. Then he peers at her, holding her close to his face. "Gracie," he whispers. "I'm Jiddo." Grandpa. She waves a pink hand, twists his cheek, and he chortles with delight. "She will tear off my face!" The house goes humid with the scent of garlic and tomato, outside is a wintry gray vapor. It's the first time in a week I've been able to look at my writing, shuffle notes. I feel like myself for a few minutes, settling back in. It's not writing, but the paper feels good in my hands, familiar as the shape of my face or the sound of my voice.

Dad, Mom, and Scott are on the couch, sacked out in front of the TV while Gracie snoozes in her basket. The grape leaves simmer, gently reheating; outside, a drizzle brushes dust off the palm leaves. It's the sort of moment that I'd package if I could: a gumdrop, postage stamp. The kind of day that makes optimists say, Hey, now This is okay. I got this.

"Grow," Scott commands three-week-old

Gracie. "Grow!" He pushes back his un-washed hair so it sticks up like feathers. "I don't know what to do with this. When can I take her kayaking?" Once again, she's doz-ing in a patch of sunlight on the carpet. "What do people do with babies?" he mut-ters. "What's their deal? They're like pet rocks."

"Houseplants."

When she sleeps, I backslide, puttering at my desk, consciousness veering off toward the novel I've been working on. Every now and then, I creep to the door to spy on her sleep, curious and impatient, like a kid peer-ing through the oven door. I go into our bathroom, stare at my sleep-drained reflec-tion; dream-shocks shake my bones. "I have a daughter," I inform the mirror. Day and night drift past our window, unconnected to our lives — we are awake or sleeping at all kinds of hours. We hustle between bottles and reading, bottles and writing, bottles and Internet — pushing back our own naps — pure madness! I'm so tired my mind feels foamy, my eyeballs burnt crispy, conscious-ness drifts away on the breeze. The ache behind my eyes sinks into my head, every-thing sagging. This was the easy time.

After a few weeks of coasting, she really wakes up.

Now the baby is implacable, demanding with new, wild screams that something must be done. She glares, hands slashing the air. We take turns walking around, bouncing, carrying her pressed to our chests and she shrieks over our shoulders. A few hours later, she's fast asleep. We anxiety-laugh and compare her to a coma victim crossed with a car alarm. She sleeps stonily, sinking below the surface, then bursts awake crying, screaming with remarkable volume. She blasts thoughts right out of my head, so I feel physically sped up, in a brainless state of emergency.

Is this completely normal? It's been more than forty years since I last lived with a baby, but I don't think so. Her bottle comes under scrutiny. After each feeding, she tucks in her chin, stiffens, wails. We try making some elaborate homebrewed stuff. We try anti-gas, gluten-free, hypoallergenic formulas. One of the pediatrician's nurses, a young woman from Barbados, slips something into my hand — a jar with a smeared label: Gripe Water. "This will do the trick," she murmurs. I sniff it and sample a bit: sweet, with an herbal scent like lemongrass and rosemary. Tilting the eyedropper, we dribble some into Gracie's mouth. No change. I research infant ailments online.

We prop her on pillows, slant her crib, lift her head. We hold her upright, at an angle, tipped up against a shoulder, put her crib on the running washing machine, turn on a hair dryer; we drive her through the streets of Coral Gables. She cries and cries. I read books about colic, try every pointer about using rockers, breathing *shshshsh* in her ears, lowering the lights. From time to time we'll hit on a small hope: Sometimes she'll settle when I carry her snug in a sling. Scott finds that if we swaddle her just right, from head to toe, tight as a cigar in one of her blankets, her crying tapers off. I learn to hold her wrapped, head propped on my shoulder, to feed her strictly upright, across my chest. But still, after most feedings, a storm of wailing shivers through the walls of our house, turns the air blue; we stash earplugs in our pockets for the worst of it.

When Gracie is seven weeks old, my friend Damaris calls to check up on us. "Is it wonderful? Are you over the moon?" she asks.

In the backseat of the car, Gracie is howling. I mash my palm against my non-phone ear. A sheaf of typed pages sits on my lap, a partial manuscript — I carry it around like a good-luck charm. "Maybe ask me that again in another month," I say with a weak laugh.

"What?" Damaris is horrified. She doesn't have children herself, but she'd watched me go step by step, working through the whole adoption process. "What do you mean?"

"No, no, we're fine. We will be fine." It would be truer to say that we're still finding out about each other, still learning who each of us is. But at two months, it seems we ought to know more than we do.

In this time after Gracie's birth, it feels as if nothing of my former self remains. Several of our child-free acquaintances make themselves scarce — perhaps afraid that I'll ramble on about diapers and bottles or I'll make them hold the baby. Another writer friend in Portland, also a mother, reassures me: "It's going to happen. All kinds of things — it's just going to shift."

"Will they go back again — the things?"

"Some will and some won't. But in the long run, it's going to be fine."

Scott, who's been up and down tending to our daughter half the night, sleeps through the mornings. I get up with Gracie. Often, she will cry and cry, her body screwing into a twist, so loud my eardrums whang back and forth. I miss my slovenly old mornings — lazing in bed, thinking of nearly nothing but the walls, the birdsong, the pool. I wrote before I did anything else, dipping into the residue of last night's dreams. Oh, what a creampuff life! Gracie lies on her back scowling, limbs floating in midair. I distract her by building things, Lego boxes and block archways that she gleefully attempts to bash. I make sock puppets, talking silverware, dancing shoes. Try not to look at the clock, not to think about time I might spend writing. Do not wonder if I'm truly meant to be a mother. Knock the wooden balls down the fretwork, replace the puzzle cutouts, dress the doll. Did James Joyce spend his days with babies? Did Yeats rush around trying to calm his infant? Or was it always the wives?

I'm haunted by a shadow-self — the person I was before I became a mother. The old habits come with me — ideas about doing what I want, when I want: How powerfully I craved freedom — a child under a doting, overbearing father; how hard it is to let even a bit of it go. My friend Laura and I walk to the outdoor trattoria nine blocks from the house. I push Gracie's carriage in the afternoon light, listening to the round, clear syllables that rise from my baby like soap bubbles. I've brought plastic keys, bottles of formula, a diaper bag. We sip iced tea under a leaf-dappled table. But as soon as our food arrives, something shifts. Perhaps it's the ravishing aroma of butter, garlic, and tomato, or the blandness of the bottle. She kicks and lets out a wail. I scoop her up, hum, strumming her back, and for a moment she settles into my arms.

Then Gracie kicks again, her crying intensifies. I stand with her and sense the other diners lowering their forks, faces turning. I don't let myself look back, afraid of what I might see. I try to pace and soothe her, but her crying grows steadily louder, verges on screaming. I haven't had a full night's sleep in weeks — I can't remember what it is to sleep. Crazy notions occur to me, thoughts bounce in and out of my rattled brain. As I pat her back, murmur into her ear, stroll between tables, for some reason I flash on the weird echo between *ambivalence* and *bivalve:* I think, a clam is the metaphor for indecision, closed into its shell. That's why they say happy as a clam, isn't it? — that solitude.

Laura takes and bounces her, and for a few blessed, distracted moments Gracie seems to quiet, but then no, the loud wail rises again, shattering the peace, unceasing. "Please sit, eat," I beg Laura. I would beg everyone around us to eat if I could. Please, pretend this isn't happening. I shoulder the baby, patting, and begin walking again, cut between the tables and go out. She doesn't start to calm until we're several blocks away. We walk and walk, her soft breaths against my chest. Gradually she curls into a snooze, cat-tongues of breath under my neck. As soon as I risk returning to our table, she awakens with a start, shrieking, her body twisting. All conversation around us stops as her screams ignite the air. Everyone here is a better, more capable parent — I'd known it all along. I am sweating, face hot, my heart hammers on my ribs; such public exposure, such a primal sense of failure. I should've known. I'd had no idea.

"Please." I wave a card at the waiter. "Can you box everything?" I gather my baby and we rush together, away from the tables and flowers and chattering people. The air colored a deep particulate blue, full of crying. We move so quickly — fleeing, all thoughts flown out of my head.

A social worker from the agency checks up on us when our baby is a few months old. It's one of Gracie's bad days: Swaddling and upright bottles and bouncing and coo-ing have little effect. Fabienne tries to

181

soothe our shrieking girl, wandering with her all over the house without luck. After not a lot of time, she hands her back. "I just think that new parents have intense first babies," she says, eyes down as she writes things on a clipboard. "Might be you're trying too hard. Maybe you're making her nervous."

I leave a note on a social media site: "Crying after every bottle — what can we do?" Dozens of parents send back consoling thoughts, pointing out that it's not entirely strange: Babies cry. "It's one of their few defenses," a father writes. "It scares tigers away." I read every comment, wishing someone could just sprinkle some fairy dust over my head; there is none.

A neighbor's three-year-old comes over with dolls and a stuffed monkey and dances them around the crib; the baby is quiet but keeps a close, skeptical eye on him. "She like dance monkeys," he tells me. "But you can't stop."

One morning, I take her out in her carriage. Often she enjoys this, lapsing into a mesmerized contentment, but today, after a few blocks, she starts screaming like she's trying to turn inside out. We pivot and head right back, but Scott is midmorning napping after a long, broken night. We can't go into the small house while she's shrieking and I can't keep wheeling her around, assaulting the neighbors. My brain feels wooden. I park her in the shade behind the house, go inside, and close the French doors. Staring through the glass at the stroller, I feel my breath whirling. I want to scream just as loud as the baby. Tears squeeze out of the corners of my eyes. *Not equipped,* I think. *Not equipped.*

One of Bud's favorite stories about my babyhood is about how he liked to threaten to throw me out of the window when I'd scream. As a kid, this cracked me up. "DAD. You didn't mean it."

"I did mean it," Bud said. "I wanted to. I would have. That window, right there."

My grandmother's solution to all problems of immoderation, from crying children to upset stomachs to bouts of wild giddiness, was a tablespoon of Kümmel — a nightmarish Germanic liquor of caraway and fumes. The taste of it was so shocking it was almost sufficient in itself to make children behave. "Slip it right into the baby bottle," she advised. "Clears things right up."

It seemed the only answer was outright surrender or alcohol. After a few moments with forehead against the window, I go back outside; I pick up my shrieking baby and rock and hum and rock and hum and she howls. None of us knows what to do, I think, and perversely, this gives me heart. None of us is equipped.

Our pediatrician asks which of us needs the checkup when we arrive for her next appointment, each of us red-eyed, the baby glaring and squirming. Dr. Toledo looks her over, pronounces her otherwise healthy, and jots something on a pad. "There's this ring of muscle — it holds in stomach contents? Sometimes it's kind of goofed up when they're first born. It takes awhile to straighten itself out. They get this acid-reflux thing. So, yeah. You're going to get a *lot* of crying." She smiles as she hands over the prescription. "I guess you already figured that part out."

I'm wary of medicine and doctors: My shaman-aunt Aya used to point at lab coats and say, "Like butchers. Only the butchers are cheaper." But we're ready to try anything, so I slip Gracie a dropper of the stuff. Something the doctor called an "H2 blocker." We wait. As the day goes on, we forget to wait. I notice evening sounds that I haven't heard in months: nightingales, the neighbor whistling for her cats, an ice-cream truck. I notice more of everything. Gracie's gray-blue eyes have deepened, over the weeks, into a rich brown. Her hair is a silky flutter. That night, I realize something is happening — it's as if there's a window, a glisten of contentment, through which we may, at last, reach each other. Her hands swim up toward my eyes, fan through the ends of my hair. Scott hums his cheek over hers — perhaps she feels the haze of stubble — a misty smile rises to her face. Could it be? Her first true smile — of pleasure or recognition or surprise, the first glint of our deep swimmer rising toward the surface. It spills through me, love like something growing wild, petals ticking open, offering its spiral, twining around our limbs. I remember this feeling — it was there, at the first instant of seeing her, on the first day of her life — and even before then, somehow, months before her birth. Perhaps it has always been in us, a rain forest, deep rooted and whole.

As soon as we begin dribbling purple drops onto her tongue, the screaming stops. Her crying subsides, she sleeps for longer periods. She laughs. We start in on new kinds of endeavor.

Dinner is a two-person operation: One of us holds and plays with Gracie while the other cuts our food and offers it up — bite for you, bite for me. We sit across from each other at the V of our couch, wedging Gracie between us. Our daughter tracks the progress of food from plate to mouth, pouting when we bring out her bottle. At six months, we give her a little rice cereal, a thin gruel with milk. Holding my breath, I spoon a dot of the cereal between her lips; she pushes it out with her tongue. I nudge a bit back in and a few particles finally slip down. Her eyes widen, food dribbling from the corners of her mouth. My heart thumps against my rib cage. It's a kind of enchantment, watching someone's first bite of food. By the third meal, Gracie opens her mouth when she sees the doll-size spoon, calling out vowel sounds as if describing tastes of things. The rice doesn't splash and burn her throat the way her milky diet had. Her sleep grows deeper. Soon, we are just about making it from one end of the evening to the other, having luscious, forgotten dreams. Oh, sleep.

As the pale buds of baby teeth emerge, Gracie's meals take on flavors, primary colors. We start with the unsurprising pureed things: applesauce, banana, squash, peas. Soon, it's mashed bits of whatever we're eating: olives, chili, sausage, lemon, garlic, Camembert. Sometimes I have to remind myself to offer her bites, to not assume she won't like it. So this is what it means to learn one another, making a first tentative study of taste, rejection, and desire. Easy. She samples with abandon, as if making up for lost time. She gums a sour pickle or grimaces at a creamy sauce with horseradish, then wants more. It's one of her earliest words: "More. More!" Soon there will be baking, but not yet. I try to set aside the sugar bowl, fearful of its long, bright shadow. After I sprinkle cinnamon on her rice cereal, she waves her arms for it, ecstatic. She opens her mouth as wide as she can, bird-style, giving herself over to new pleasure. Cooking and eating swaying in their balance: Good as it is to offer pleasure, it's just as important to learn how to accept it.

CHAPTER EIGHT:
ASKING QUESTIONS, LOOKING CLOSELY

Dave wants only the truth these days. My father-in-law is the last of the great question-askers. He wants to know, to see what's there, to peel back the veil. He asks people just about anything that occurs to him. He does so with such guileless curiosity that you could be halfway through your answer before you realize he's asking for intimate information on relationships, personal grooming, or digestive outcomes. He is just as forthcoming about his own details, casually revealing which of his children he'd let fall from the changing table, his past marital indiscretions, something he'd glimpsed in the toilet bowl — so relaxed, he might be discussing the weather report.

One night at the dinner table — several months after the grape-feeding incident and several years before our daughter will be born — Bud was watching Dave out of the corner of his eye. He and Mom had arrived in Orlando with us to celebrate Christmas with my new in-laws. We were all spending a few days at their house, getting to know one another. Beginning with salad and progressing through to dishes of ice cream, Dave asked Bud why Iraq had invaded Iran, whether Muslims believed there are two hundred naked virgins waiting in heaven, if he really ate goat eyeballs, the meaning and historical context of his family name, and what the Palestinians were always so hot under the collar about.

After dinner, Bud pulled me outside the front door as everyone else was moving toward bed. "How well you know this guy, Scotty's dad?" he hissed. It was a crackling cold December night, the lawns of Orlando frosted with moonlight. "Is he with someone?"

"What now?"

"You know." Bud glanced at the lighted windows. "CIA"

I couldn't keep the exasperation out of my voice. "Bud, for real?"

"He asks so many questions. Americans don't ask that many," he said. He'd never met anyone quite so straightforwardly curious before.

■ ■ ■ ■

When the doctor tells Dave there's no cure, he listens, clear-eyed, nodding. Once again, he tries to peel back layers, to look as directly as he can at what is happening. Propped in a clean white hospital bed, he says, "I keep thinking I have to go through all those stages of — what are they? Fear? Anger? Maybe I'm just stuck in denial. How do you know?" Outside, around the parking garage, there is a light perfume from distant orange groves. Whiffs of citrus seem to cross these rooms like reports from another world. He stares out his window past a row of palm trees, his engineer's mind at work. For years he was an applications engineer for Techtronix; postretirement, he's maintained a medical robot that simulates patient symptoms for nursing students. "Is it weird to say I just really think this is interesting?"

Dave's children lamented his Vulcan approach to life, this lack of fuzzy fatherly emotion. But having grown up with all emotion and little clarity, I find his style brisk and refreshing. The idea that one might say precisely what one is thinking, and welcome, without judgment or criticism, that same precision from others, is a novelty to me —

even a joy. Throughout the procedure, he quizzes the doctor performing his thoracentesis — lung draining — and asks to inspect the cannula. Afterward, the specialist rubs his glasses on his lab coat, saying, "Patients generally just close their eyes. Not this one."

I would have closed my eyes. It's hard to look. You get so used to life, so surrounded and protected and shielded by the brightness of the morning, the incandescence of childhood just around the last corner — a state you emerged from just yesterday. How to imagine that such a time comes to a close?

Ten years earlier, I watched in fragments my grandmother pass away, as if peeping between my fingers — a visit here, a visit there. Even during her last days in the hospital, I was telling myself stories about visiting for the next holiday and also the one after that. But Gram was writing her own story, while she drifted between the wires and tubes, the busy white world clicking off its seconds on the heart monitor. We found it afterward under her bed, scratched on the back of some doctor's medical notes: "My dear family. Please let me go to live with Jesus Christ." Steady devotion, foundational as the earth. Love comes with its aggravations, and still it's not possible to completely let go of it.

Mom had called to tell us that Gram had gone, but she couldn't finish any of the sentences. Dad came back on the line to explain things. "She's okay," he said. "She misses her mom now."

Bud was young when he lost his parents. His father passed on when Bud was a teenager and his mother when he was in his early twenties, living in the States. He grew up in such a crowded family that he never had enough of his parents to begin with. Our grief seemed a little exotic and outsized to him, as if some improbable new beast had entered the room, moved all the furniture. "What? She was old," he'd said. "Death is good. It's fine. Better than being crazy and crackled." I couldn't accept things as plainly as he did, and I wrestled with a sense of disbelief: Grace couldn't be gone. She would never do that! It felt more like she was missing than dead. Gone into hiding.

At her funeral, I had asked at the last moment to be a pallbearer. I almost didn't — I wondered whether it would seem strange — but Mom had said, "No, go tell them." I could just see my grandmother pointing to the center of her chest, saying, "You can always know what to do if you feel down here, like a knuckle." The men looked nonplussed for a moment before one of the funeral home staff bowed out. The weight of her coffin was a powerful comfort, hard and solid, something to press against, instead of the lightness of death. It was like a shared secret, the pressure of a hand, an old memory — something only a few of us would know. It helped me begin to feel what had happened, to know this loss — not only in my mind but also in my arms and legs and back. My father knelt by the side of the coffin and opened his hands to the heavens, crying for his old adversary.

Over the course of a year, there's been a lot of movement in and out of that white bed, a good deal of testing, dosing, and treatment, to buy us a few scanty months. Eventually, Dave stops going back in. At his seventieth birthday party, he receives visitors at home as he lies propped in bed beside an oxygen tank. The bed has become his house and table. Here he watches TV, socializes, reads the newspaper. Boxes of cookies and bowls with grape stems float across the bedsheets. Our three-month-old daughter snoozes in the guest room, among the coats. Bud and Mom come into my father-in-law's bedroom. Bud holds both of Dave's hands and Dave says, "I always think about those red grapes." Bud cracks his favorite worst joke, "I don't care what they say about you, Dave. You're a great guy." We bring Gracie in to finally meet her other grandfather. We settle her against his side; she burrows between his arm and ribs, companionably, still half-asleep. His eyes tick over her soft form. A hundred questions he wants to ask her, but he doesn't have the breath. "Hello, Gracie," he manages. "How do you do?"

The water is a waxy, crinkling light far down the green slope, dotted with birds and turtles. Scott, Gracie, and I take a table out on the back porch, under an umbrella that sheds blue light. Once on this same marshy slope, my father-in-law gasped and pointed at an alligator just inches from my foot. I choked on my own yelp, jerking backward, before I realized the thing was cement (a harder distinction to make than you might think). Dave cried with laughter; later, I was required to pose for a picture with my foot on its head.

Julie's Lakeside — of the crooked floors, the fish sandwiches, and the live music — has been one of our Orlando mainstays.

Lately, we've been going in between hospital and doctor visits, reassured by the little old place, its broke-down familiarity an antidote to bedsheets and sick rooms.

Today the singer's electric Hammond wakes Gracie in her carriage. Her eyes fix on him. In a few more years, we'll find that if there is music, Gracie will insist someone get out there with her and move wildly. I will stomp among cloggers and swing to reggae in clouds of three-year-olds and do freeform movement to cover bands on the beach. She will grow up with her jiddo clapping his hands at her, hooting, "Dance! Dance!" Now she waves her arms at the drum box, so I stand, holding her, and we bob around the patio. The singer half-watches us, mild and distracted. This man has entertained multitudes of children, has sung these songs so many times he no longer hears them — they must loop through his days, natural as exhaling.

He leans into a microphone, giving us the usual South Florida medley — Jimmy Buffett, Beach Boys, Beatles. Then the atmosphere shifts, some molecule seems to enter the air, and there's a pause, as if something is being reconsidered. Then he begins singing, "I see trees of green, red roses too. . . ." Less adorned, less adamantly upbeat, his voice is nearly rueful; it's the sort of singing that makes you stop eating and listen. In the midst of scraping chairs and the clatter of silverware, the performer, who holds a mic in one hand and braces himself with the other, is singing to Gracie. We drift alongside the song. "The bright blessed day . . . the dark sacred night. . . ."

I lower my head, annoyed by myself, already feeling a catch in my throat. The words, about witnessing the beauty of the world, slide along to a childlike melody, saying, no one notices, no one else sees, and children grow up, flowers close, the beauties slip away while you're not looking. Bikers, hard-tanned locals, snowbirds from Jersey, Ohio, Quebec chatter around us, waving cigarettes between their nails, the air filled with talk and cologne. "Nobody loves Florida," Scott said to me. "Nobody stays here long enough to know what it is." But the song — that almost no one is listening to — seems written for this very place, this bug-bitten, over-hot state, ragged and fringed, lovely as any frontier. My eyes are pinched by stupid tears. I count my daughter among the catalog of beautiful things: the water, the sky, the swish of her arms through the air, even the fact of this moment — that we all happen to be alive at the same time, all sharing this glimpse of daylight. Maybe a few of us also share the same regret — that we can't seem to remember to keep looking. That we return to our own kinds of blindness each day. We ask few questions, turn away, and forget each other's names. Not just beauty is lost on us — all of it is. My father-in-law won't get to see his granddaughter walk or laugh or hear her call his name.

Now Scott holds Gracie before him and she reaches toward his face, grappling with eyebrows and ears. He laughs, lets her tug fistfuls of hair. When she cries out at night, he races out of his sleep, cradles her, naps on the floor by her crib. I see Dave in my husband's patience and rare gentleness and unbreakable gaze. It's startling to me, these other sorts of fathers, calm, easy — so different from my own — yet all of them true, abiding fathers.

We watch the man sing with such purity, "I see friends shaking hands, saying how do you do? They're really saying, I love you. . . ." What a singer this man must have been, before the drum box and the tip jar, before his voice had turned so far inward, missing a place or a time that was once splendid but has gone now and will never come again.

■ ■ ■ ■

Weeks later, Bud and Mom join Scott,
Gracie, and me at Dave's memorial service.
It is dim, cool, and very crowded, voices
rising like incense, the scent of shared
memory. I hold our baby while we sing
"Amazing Grace," tuck my nose into her
hair, and close my eyes.

CHAPTER NINE:
LEGACY

Daddy knows all kinds of good places to eat: takeout chicken wings in the car — tossing bones back into the box with the uneaten wings, which Mama finds amusing yet mildly repulsive. Grazing at the market — a dusty grape here, a dried mango slice there — as he picks up the last-minute groceries. And there is something Daddy calls "relaxing dinner," which means plates spread over the coffee table and aimed at the TV.

Mama likes tables. Gracie helps set the table, plates teetering, one at a time, between her fingers. She folds the paper towels into "napkins," an assortment of random tiny shapes. She prefers to cut up her own food, but not necessarily to eat it. Then begins the dinner conversation:

"Mama, tell me bout when you were a bad little girl."

I scour my memory for a story I haven't

already told three times. If it's sweet or nostalgic, she stops me. "Is there a bad? Put in the bad."

Daddy and I protest that we can only remember good, happy, obedient-child stories; she becomes impatient. "No. Bad story. When you were bad."

These requests remind me of the years I attended Catholic school, first to third grades, the dark minutes spent inside the confessional, the imperative to recall all those bad stories and hand them over, like dues, to the authorities. But I couldn't remember my sins, not in any satisfying narrative form. Perhaps I just didn't want anyone to dictate how I told my stories — instead, I offered the priests imaginary, spiced-up transgressions:

"I'm a secret agent from another planet."

"I can fly. I look at people's heads from up high."

"I talk to dogs. They know me."

I tell Gracie about making up sins in the confessional, how I first became a fiction writer at Our Lady of Solace. "More!" she hollers, hands in small fists on the table. "More stories about that."

Enough with the stories, we say, food's getting cold. I suggest we hold hands and say grace.

"Say Gracie?"

"*Grace.* It's like a kind of thank-you. A prayer."

"What's that?" Her round eyes dark as plums.

"A story," Scott says. "It's for when you eat together at a table."

"About me?"

"Yes," I say, "About you."

"Tell me that story. Tell me the Grace."

We try to explain about prayer, but we've gotten out of practice. "It's like talking to God, or, I don't know, heaven, or maybe like the universe, and telling what you're thinking about, or feeling. Or hoping for," Scott concludes.

"Like this?" She spreads her hands on the table and closes her eyes. "Dear Jiddo," she begins, addressing Bud. "Please I want a really, really big doggie. I love you. Love, Gracie." She looks at Scott. "Is that a pray?"

He nods. "Now say 'Amen.' "

"Amen." She thinks about it, then adds, "A-girl."

You know she was from Bethlehem; her father was a minister, an Arab Anglican. You know they were refugees, that they found sanctuary with your grandfather's family in Jordan. You know she was quite young —

he was just a bit older; he liked to enjoy himself, to drink and invite and fall in love — and she was cultivated, educated, meant for college and a loftier life. But your grandfather's family, with their old Bedouin roots, had land and prosperity and a noble, long-lived name. They were a safer harbor. You know that after they married, she collected a library of books, slowly, over the years, a hedge against dispossession and exile. You know she went on to bear at least seven boys and one girl, though you've been told there were more, possibly many more. You know that her image seems to stand right up out of every photograph you've seen of her; she looks solarized, separated from the others by a thin black line, as if limned by the force of her own will. But with all that, you will never know what her voice sounded like or what the sweep of her hair felt like or what she might have felt about giving her life to all those clamorous children. She died when she was forty-eight — though, in the rare pictures, she looks older. She had gestational diabetes and passed away after your father had emigrated to the States. In your father's unmedical opinion, she died not *in* childbirth — not from one — but *from* childbirth, giving birth and raising children in general — too many children. "They killed her," he says, as if he weren't one of them.

You imagine her when she was still young and lithe, walking into her library, shedding sadness like bits of skin. You imagine the release she felt between her ribs; in such places, you've felt it unlock in yourself. A space of rare air, diffuse light, where the voices of children can be heard only distantly, through a wall of books.

Years ago, outside one of the abandoned Crusader castles in Jordan, in an empty, sand-blown quarter, from out of nowhere, a Bedouin with burnt skin and green eyes approached you, murmuring your grandmother's name: shaken, seeing her ghost in your face. He'd met her when she was newly arrived in the country; he worked for your grandfather's family but brought that girl fresh milk from his goats and carried her memory with him like a locket.

You know that she loved her children because your father had learned to love so well. He is domineering, erratic, and volatile, but also affectionate, doting, outlandishly proud. She must have loved them enormously. But what a struggle for a young woman, a refugee in a strange country, so many children. You wonder as well if there weren't moments — fleeting, quicker even than thought — when she was leaving the soft, book-lined walls, the crimson Persian rugs, the high, rich light thrown in from the slotted windows, this child and that one crying out her name — that she didn't also wish them all away.

Two a.m., sleep and night braid deep-sea strands. Rising slowly toward a beam of sound, I drag the covers back, baby crying in the blue-black darkness. At four or five a.m., I return to bed and lie there, too tired to work, unable to get back to sleep. The big moon eases toward my window and gazes in. This is the hour of visitations: wondering over the grandmother I didn't know, the missing one. Thoughts of her come in the softest part of the night, when I feel disoriented, cut open. Her silence is its own lesson, warning: Never stop speaking.

But I haven't written. Not for two, three, four months: This becomes frightening to me. I've lost time at various points in my writing career. There are years between my first and second published books: I spent half a decade — hundreds, thousands, of discarded pages — on a novel that never cohered. Of course, I wasn't just writing — those years were also taken up with teaching. The classes, the advising, the meetings upon meetings, days when my office call-waiting hopped from one request to the next. The crooked path of a writing life: a series of starts and stops, not enough money, too much teaching or journalism. On top of this was my penchant for writerly experiments — I wove science fiction, mysteries, history into the fiction — piled up as many unpublished manuscripts as published books. Heaps of unread work.

The most recent experiment happened a few years before Gracie's birth, when a children's-books editor sent a note. She'd read my novel *Crescent,* which contains an ongoing fable, and thought I should try my hand at a narrative for young people. There was a story I liked to tell one of my young nieces, about a mirror world filled with living reflections — something I secretly imagined telling to my own someday-daughter. I tried getting it down — a fantasyland filled with talking objects and flying witches and hidden stairs. But writing it, fastening it in print, changed the story somehow. I kept rewriting and second-guessing, shifting it from fantasy into psychological drama and back again. I asked anyone I could corner if they would read the pages. After three years of rewrites and rounds of kindly critiques, the story felt distorted and unmanageable, and I couldn't bear to look at it anymore. I shelved it in mourning: I'd published three books but began to feel afraid I'd forgotten how to do it.

One night, as I'm waiting for Gracie to slip off to sleep against my chest, I begin thinking about a novel that I'd started back in the fall then put down after my daughter's birth. This story is a bit mysterious, even disturbing to me, about a woman's near-destruction after her child has run away. As I stroke Gracie's back, I wonder whether it's unnatural to have started writing this in the months before my own daughter would be born. There's always been this perversity in me to write down things that I ought to avoid. Perhaps it's a way to keep from being too consumed by certain fears — a warding-off. My grandmother Grace had a tremendous knack for saying things out loud that most people only thought, and the absence of my other grandmother's voice was its own cautionary reminder. Shouldn't you look at and think about exactly the things that frighten you the most? I'd handwritten a stack of pages by the time Gracie was born. Now the story begins to reinhabit me; the characters stand up, speaking, re-arranging furniture.

Still, my eyes glaze as I sit at my desk, concentration dissolves into drowsiness. You're told: Sleep when the baby sleeps. But those quiet hours are the only times the mind seems to fit back into its skull. I want to be awake. I should work, I tell myself over and over. Now's my chance! I recall a writer once saying that becoming a parent was good for her work — the time constraints moved her toward discipline and more orderly habits. "If my son was going to be asleep for three hours each day, I knew I'd darn well better use that time and get serious."

Get serious! I scold myself.

The words slip away from me, threads on the surface of the eye. I'm paralyzed, creaking, sleep-deprived, and on alert, waking every few hours, anticipating Gracie's first cry from the crib. I miss simple thought, the unoccupied hours in which I could gradually piece together stories. That state of unencumbrance is what I imagine my missing grandmother had wanted — the space, of the mind and house — to lose herself in books. If you have a baby to care for, there are these moments, each time she cries out, in which your mind peels into two pieces, a split twig: You go to her, but you must leave your books, your space, and the sound of your own voice.

Sometimes the idea of having a baby seems ridiculous and Promethean, like flying too close to the sun — an act of wild hubris. Who dares to think they should be parents?

Gracie is a few months old when we go out to dinner with friends at a favorite café, located in a bookshop. In the central courtyard, the café is ringed by plants and trees, a small grove. Today, there are also spotlights, cameras, and microphones set up in a circle. It turns out the writer Tom Wolfe is in town being interviewed. Margaria, one of the friends we're meeting, an editor and critic, offers to introduce us.

Here's a vestige of my former life, of days of coffeehouses and readings and conversations. Yes, this will be fine: baby on this side, author over there. Gracie has fallen asleep on me, and the main objective is always to do whatever will keep her sleeping. So there's a baby nestled in my arm as we wait for a break in the interview. Mr. Wolfe is resplendent in his white suit. He looks so bright and clean, like the song about edelweiss, almost mystical — as though he lived inside a white sheen. Our friend moves forward to greet him and, as she does, my glance happens to fall to my wrist, where I spot a fleck of mustard.

Huh, I think. That's weird.

Because none of us has been eating mustard, there's no mustard on the table, so why is there mustard on my wrist?

I move to wipe it, surreptitiously, on my jeans — there's just a dot, but I must take care not to leave a tiny smear on Tom Wolfe's sleeve. As I move my left arm, I notice another speck of mustard on my other wrist, just where it curls around Gracie's bundled form. Tom Wolfe is turning now, our friend's hand on his forearm, to be introduced, his hand rising toward mine, as it occurs to me — with a slow, stop-motion, dawning horror — that the dot of mustard is actually more like a stripe, a banner of yellow gleaming as I follow it along the length of my forearm. I understand, finally, so slowly as to convey the terrible depth of my inexperience, that it isn't mustard.

I burst into a sprint at the moment that our friend is saying, "I'd like to introduce. . . ."

Gracie lets out a heart-splitting scream as we run across the crowded courtyard, streaming yellow fecal splatter. We crash through the bathroom door. There in the mirror, I see an outline of Gracie's body like a crime-scene chalk drawing in diarrhea across my chest, throat, and blouse. There is shit everywhere — coating the insides of my arms, ribboned down the front of my pants. I pull the blanket away from Gracie and it splashes into the sink as she shrieks, distraught.

Scott rushes into the ladies' room behind me. "OH MY GOD, WHAT IS THAT?"

I've turned the faucets on and we have to shout to hear ourselves over the screaming and water and the thump of our own panic. "BABY CRAP."

"Oh, God. Oh, my God." Scott tries to hold her as she writhes away from the tepid stream. There are poo splashes and splatters all over us, the counter, and the wailing baby. At this moment, a stately Coral Gables matron enters and takes in this scene, her hand flying to the pearls at the base of her throat. Scott and I freeze like she's pointed a gun. The woman pulls her chin in, red lips an asterisk, and says at last, backing out of the room, "I'll wait."

When we finally dare return to the courtyard, Tom Wolfe has dematerialized. We are soaked. Gracie's skin is rosy and clean. We sit and eat dinner quickly, before anything else can happen.

■ ■ ■ ■

Three, four, five months pass and I've barely written a word. Editors contact me, wanting blurbs for new manuscripts. I write to one, "I've lost your galley and I haven't washed my hair in a week. Don't wait for me," as if I've crash-landed in the desert. I look with despair upon the heaps of unfinished manuscripts on my desk. I now share an office with my husband. My old office contains a crib, a changing table, and perhaps thirty-three stuffed animals. Everything I write sounds flat, shattered as an old mosaic. Gracie takes two uneven naps from eleven to twelve and three to five. Three free hours a day. Three hours — that should be plenty! What's wrong with me? I berate myself, thinking of the people with multiple jobs and big families who must do their writing at night or far too early in the morning. I think of my absent grandmother, her house swirling with children — and out in the rocky fields beyond, herds of goat and sheep waiting to be fed and milked. I write a few sentences and fall into a trance at the computer. I wake at Gracie's call, face pressed against my keyboard.

■ ■ ■ ■

Each outing reveals undiscovered countries.

Today, for example. I hear the *whoosh* before I see it.

Gracie stands frozen, little hands still curled in the shape of the plastic container she was recently holding.

For a moment it's as if my eyes refuse to focus, refuse to take in the Pollock splatter of mango-colored slush all over white marble. Somehow the stuff has traveled amazing, inconceivable distances — from espadrilles on Doric column to Hermès display case to Tiffany silver. One tremendous orange iceberg melts at our feet. The mall has transformed into another dimension, another planetoid, the far side of Mars, perhaps.

We had ducked into the chic department store for their restroom. After that, we dawdled our way, disheveled and food-stained, through Women's Shoes, the stroller a glorified purse-holder — the toddler won't stay in it: Its wheels move too quickly through interesting places. Then we'd made our way past the sporty $500 designer-sneakers area and into the snazzier section where a salesman once explained to my husband that a pair of feather-covered stilet-tos were "inside shoes," meant never to touch pavement. That was around the time when I heard Gracie say, "Uh oh."

The enormous, devious, plastic take-out container lies on its side a few feet away. She wanted to hold the cup and I, mania-cally enough, let her do so. My daughter's eyes roll from the cup to me: She's waiting to find out how one reacts to this sort of thing. I've heard children will look at their parents' faces after an injury to learn if they're in pain or not, if they should freak out or not. They watch and adjust, calibrate the intensity of the tears or the laughter. A parent must step outside herself, gather her wits, recall that she no longer simply reacts but models, that someone nearby is study-ing every breath. It takes all my nerve not to throw up my hands and sidle away, whistling. It's our mess now; we've made it together.

"Ah ha!" I manage, berating myself. Tricked again by a plastic container. "Well, well!" I try to sound somehow interested, as if this is a kind of scientific experiment or medical study. "Look at that." Her face relaxes as she studies the scene. "Wuh!" she says, almost proudly.

I pinch the cap between two fingers and

try to scrape melted smoothie back into the cup in what can only be described as an exercise in futility. We'd already, somehow, used up the twenty-seven napkins I'd dug out of the dispenser before we'd left the coffee shop. Outside of a mop and pail, this situation is irredeemable. I look around, praying one of the beautifully dressed, terrifying sales clerks is a mother.

But no one is there. In fact, there is scarcely a soul in the entire store. I can hear myself breathing. Someone, her back to us, appears to be rearranging perfume bottles at a counter about a football field away; she doesn't look over. They all apparently vacated the premises, fleeing up escalators and crouching in Men's Formal Wear, perhaps just a few seconds after the cap burst open.

I tear a page out of the notebook I keep in the despised stroller and scrawl, "SO SORRY. We had an accident." It's all I can think to do. Something about doing this reminds me of lighting candles in church with my grandmother — leaving messages in small bottles. Consciousness folds at such times — it is one in a series of moments when you discover another layer of parenting: standing together, no matter how disgraced, sharing the moment in this human project. There are a few singles in my wallet, so I throw those in as well. I fold the note into its own crude aerogram and prop it by the mess. The person who cleans this — I can almost see her bending slowly, sighing — will surely be a mother.

My parents, my grandparents — indeed, most everyone of a certain time and place — grew up within extended family. Support — emotional, material, even spiritual — was all around. As my Aunt Aya said, "The good thing about the olden times is you were never alone. The bad thing about the olden times is you were never alone." For both Bud and Gram, religion was part of this family. Bud had grown up in an Arab-Christian family, but he'd lost both parents as a young man. While in the military he converted to Islam, drawn to its codes and regulations — the sort of careful instructions — everything from diet to charity to etiquette — a boy might receive from his parents. His commanding officer, whom Bud had admired and leaned on after his own father died, had been Muslim. For Bud, Islam was a channel between America and Jordan, a touchstone to nation and identity.

Grace lived her Catholicism through rituals. The hinge in each week was a shared ride to church with a gang of old gals, a couple of her sisters, a few of her friends — all had outlasted their husbands. Sometimes I joined them to sit in the cloud of nylons and permanent waves, face powder, clip-on earrings, Sunday coats, inside allusions to bridge games and bowling league. The big church interior was dark and intense, with a grand organ, a baritone priest, slow, patient readings and hymns, occasionally shouted sermons. Afterward, we walked out into a cold, bright world, snowflakes stirring overhead, and the promise of stopping at the Russian bakery for babka.

In their turf wars, Dad let Gram have the religion. My sisters and I were raised within the church — whenever Gram visited. The notion of the mystical or metaphysical, the life beyond or divine will was always sublimated within a host melting on the tongue — the elements of body and spirit whirled around each other, entwined. You had to feed the body to polish the soul. Home from Sunday church, Gram's apartment smelled like roast beef, so rich and unvarying, you could almost taste the marrow releasing, the flour and mushrooms in the brown gravy. My grandmother said, "Ain't that a smell?"

Often, her sisters joined us: Aunt Helen in veiled hats and lacy hankies, using delicate, educated-Jersey vowels; Aunt Alyce, who couldn't hear a thing and laughed with a tremendous hoot, and who barreled everywhere but to church in a rattling, uninspected vehicle nicknamed the Deathmobile. They compared notes on mass, took themselves out for chocolate éclairs, showered each other with unlistened-to advice, and helped school and raise their pooled children. Days were built on the Sunday ride, a constant reason to be together. Church made the spiritual material, the wide world a little more manageable.

"Grace was our in-tell-ect-ual," Alyce shouted over Sunday dinner. "She had the white gloves and the prayer book."

"So refined and dainty," Helen jumped into their weekly communal boasting.

"I was always a size six, no matter what I ate," Gram said.

"Not me," Alyce boasted. "What do I care? I only dress for church."

"I don't care what you believe," my father jumped in, generally missing the gist of the conversation. "As long as you believe in something bigger than you are."

"And as long as it's Catholic," Gram added with a sniff.

■ ■ ■ ■

It's a splendid May morning, the sun burning a hole in the blue sky. A mariachi car horn bleats in the distance. Gracie and I are out for our morning stroll: I sing a passionate rendition of "Old MacDonald," trying to distract her from the humidity. Most mornings, we pass a bevy of Spanish-speaking nannies who smile and nod and conjecture as to why the gringa pushes her own baby. I admire and envy the Cuban families of Miami. They remind me of the Jordanians, the way everyone picnics and visits en masse, and if there isn't an abuela to watch the children — and often when there is — there will also be support staff. Today, one of the nannies strikes up a little conversation, starting with the basics in Spanish: *Que linda! Quanto anos tiene?* My resources extinguished, we switch to English:

"You are enjoying yourself?"

I smile, considering. "Sure. Well, I suppose. . . ."

"You do some kind of working? Beside baby?"

The air has a shiny quality, like the inside of a seashell. I push Gracie's stroller back and forth in place. "I write. I used to. I haven't since . . . ," tipping my head toward the stroller.

The woman's chin rises. She curves one hand over mine for a moment. "So you know what you do? You hire a nanny."

We live in a shoebox in Coral Gables — a famously upscale neighborhood. I'm constantly telling impressed acquaintances that we barely cling to the middle class. "We can't."

"Not live in." She shakes a finger. "Just work hours."

I shrug, arms out. "Even if we could, with our house? We'd be standing on top of each other."

"It will work." Now she squeezes my elbow. "In Cuba, my uncle is a writer. I know how it is. You have to get some help. Arrange things. You see. Even if you go in debt. You have to do it anyways — when you are happier. . . ." She shrugs. "The baby? Becomes happier, too."

Gracie begins fretting, kicking, tiny bouncing feet, complaints starting in little gusts. The woman gives me a look. "In my country, I'm psychologist. Here, I start at the bottom again. It's normal. Everyone has to start somewhere, right? That's how it is with a baby — you're starting back in the beginning — for both of you. On the floor."

When I get home, I put Gracie down; the walk and the sunlight have made her dopey. She drifts on her mattress, face down, bottom up, knees curled in like a pill bug. For once, I think I will also take a nap, but I just stare at the lunar map of the ceiling. I muse over the nanny-psychologist's advice to get help. The idea of starting from the beginning — or the floor — depending on your angle. Instead, though, my mind roves around, considering: My grandmother Grace taught, but she lived with her parents and siblings — there was always someone on hand to help out with her daughter. When my mother went back to work, her teaching schedule matched our school hours. And there was my other grandmother, ensconced at home with eight children. Would she have been appalled at this weakness, the very idea of enlisting help? I see her again in that wonderful library, her private land whispering with stories, running her fingers over the spines, titles like wishes, like half-true dreams.

Her name, *Aniseh,* my father said, means "Lovely young lady. Just like your other grandmother's name." Two graces: one seen, one unseen, one heard, one silent. And yet both quite present. Both of them, I think, are telling me the same thing.

CHAPTER TEN:
THE SERVANT

The child's voice has come loose.

It is somewhere at the center of the night, a lost thing, this imploring cry: Mama, Mama, Mama.

Daddy gets up and goes to her, wandering through the nightlands. But tonight she sobs and says, Mama, Mama. And then there is nothing to do: Hand finds its way to the covers, peels them back, the warmth coming away in a soft, thick layer. Feet find their way out of dreams, midair to the floor. Pushing up, assembling bones upright, pushing against the downward currents of sleep. Push, push. Bones straightening. The rooms shifting to starboard as if in a gust of seawind. Wavering in her doorway, whisper, "Yes, Baby?"

"Mama, I'm hungry." Plaintive.

The kitchen at the other end of the nightlands, barely lit: a digital clock, a computer switch, scattered and rare dots of light, the windows of a small town in the evening. Pat the counters, half-blind, eyes nearly shut, until hand closes on something.

Back in her room, soft with the smell of sleep. "Here, Baby." Give her the opened banana.

She pulls back the covers. "Mama, come in," she murmurs.

Obey. This is who I am now: My service has sunk into me, deep down, knit to the bones, to my very name. I am hers, possession and servant. Lie down. Her head rests on my shoulder and there are the tiny sounds of eating. Neither of us speaks. We belong to each other. Within six bites, she melts back into sleep. Her hand and half a banana float on my ribs.

Both of us asleep.

But what is her title — babysitter or nanny or caretaker? She is not family or even, yet, friend.

Her name is Soledad, but she says we should call her Janet. She's twenty. She's attending Miami–Dade and wants to be a doctor someday, or a flight attendant, maybe — she is having some trouble in organic chemistry. Her hobbies include swimming and shopping online. She cooks, she tells us, ticking off her kid specialties, "macaroni and cheese — frozen and box types; chicken fingers — just frozen; and peanut butter and jelly sandwiches." Her smile draws her face into deep dimples. She comes bequeathed to us from a friend of a friend, who calls her the "Cuban Mary Poppins."

"Can you speak Spanish?" I lean forward on the couch.

She crosses her arms and legs, foot bobbing. "Like, if I totally have to?" Her mother is from Cuba, her father is Nicaraguan, and she is "one hundred percent Miami-girl."

I nod with enthusiasm, tell her about my dread of Bud's daily Arabic lessons — the rote memorization and repetition of formal phrases; his attempts to enforce our identity. I sling my legs over the couch arm, act like we're already pals, have known each other forever. Grace lounges on the couch cushions, twinkling at the new sitter. Janet pounces on her. "Look at the princess!" She lifts Gracie, nuzzling her neck. "I can't wait to have kids. I'm gonna have a million!"

She shows up for work swathed in perfume, outfitted in Miami-wear I describe to a friend as stripper casual. Clinging T-shirts with plunging necklines and Versace-esque cutouts. Miniskirts of layered fishnet with opaque leggings. Painted-on jeans, nude heels, glittery bangles, as well as baby-exciting necklaces known around here as mommy-nooses. She pushes Gracie — wailing — up the street in her stroller. Riveted to the window, we watch them amble away.

Scott puts an arm around my shoulder. "There goes our daughter with a total stranger."

I stare until they turn the corner at the end of our block and briefly consider tailing them in the car. I go to my office, sit bolt upright at my desk; next thing I know, I'm in the kitchen making pretzels.

Over the years, I've lost the habit of eating ice cream for breakfast, but my baking has only increased. And this process feels as good as a stretch — all that kneading, squashing, smashing, rolling dough on the cutting board, tying pieces into knots, throwing them in boiling water. It's one of Grace's old anxiety cures. Out of the oven, the tray of pretzels gets brushed with butter, sprinkled with coarse salt. When they return, Janet leaves Gracie in her stroller and heads straight to the kitchen. She eats three pretzels in a row, murmuring, "You made these?" During the first week with Janet, I bake pretzels every day. Very slowly, my fretting dissipates; my head wanders back to the new novel, working out questions of motivation and structure. I push the dough, fold it, push, and the mindless movements draw the thoughts forward through my arms. On the third week with our babysitter, I skip a day of baking. Janet stands in the kitchen, staring as I pour a cup of tea, and finally says, "Where are the pretzels?"

I am learning something about serving, which is that when you become a good servant, it is tempting to bow to everyone. Especially when you're new on the job. I try not to be obvious when I tidy up after her — wait till they're on their walk before collecting the dishes she leaves here and there, little piles of crumbs like the Hansel and Gretel trail. She straightens not a thing, leaves mostly ruin in her wake, and during the hours that Gracie sleeps, she stretches out on the couch, languidly clicking through shopping websites. I half-admire her; she might be a babysitter, but she is not a servant.

I stock Janet's favorite coffee, call her mother if she's caught in traffic on the way home, worry if she's forgotten her umbrella, buy her a pair of more comfortable shoes. There is also a lot of listening. Janet has personal problems. Her boyfriend has moved in with her and her family and he's "causing issues" with her mother. Her mother's own boyfriend is, she says, "a boss" who tells her to study more. Her father wants her to move back to Nicaragua and wait on him. One day she arrives red-eyed and sniffling: Her family is maybe about to be evicted. Her mother's second ex-husband is demanding an equal division of all their assets. Her mother isn't able to afford to buy his half of the house; unless she allows the ex-husband and his mother to move back in, the eight of them must go.

"Go?" I perch on the footstool across from her. "To where?"

She rubs the back of one plump hand under her nose. She has a lavish figure, her skin smooth as an olive. When she's agitated, she draws her black hair forward on to one shoulder and pulls it through her fingers as if stroking a cat. She tips back on the couch, stroking her hair, skirt inched up her plump thighs. "My mom's got a friend in Kendall with three-bedroom apartment over her garage. She says we could move in there."

But there are so many of them! Later, I wonder quietly if we should offer to let Janet sleep on our couch, and Scott smiles and says, "Absolutely not." He doesn't like the "endless problems," her "telenovela life."

For all our talking and proximity, we are still scarcely more than acquaintances. Recently, when Janet was out walking Gracie, our excitable neighbor Ines — whom Scott and I call "the neighborhood watch," came rushing over.

"Some girl has gone off with your daughter!"

"No, that's Janet. The babysitter."

Ines scowled. "She's from where, that girl?"

"Here. Hialeah."

Ines stared at me.

"Her father is from Nicaragua, her mother is Cuban."

Her scowl deepened. Ines is Cuban. "That is what she told you? With hair like that? She's some kind of Indios." She pulled down one lower lid with an index finger. "Keep an eye out."

The telenovela continues. We don't know from one day to the next if Janet will show up for work with a mascara-tracked face or even show up at all. Scott begins to say things about "moving her along." But after several months together, I'm used to her. Spending entire days with someone in your house is a lot like living with them, even if you don't know each other very well. Almost without noticing, and against my better

228

judgment, I've developed a fondness for Janet. I'd seen it in all sorts of families — it's the child with the grubby, teary face, the unemployable cousin, the trying auntie who gets the most money or help or love. The virtuous ones are too self-sustaining, too functional — what do they need? The ones with the problems always have their arms out for hugs.

Because I can't think what else to do to help, I begin making big pots of food in the afternoon and sending Janet home with bowls of pasta carbonara, meatballs, spicy chili, lentil soup. Her mother has allowed her ex-husband and Mami to move back in, and now he works with the boyfriend in his landscaping business. According to Janet, somehow they're all getting along "very lovely." But not even Mami wants to do the cooking. Through the kitchen wall, I hear the sounds of Janet singing, reading, chanting rhymes to Gracie. The minute actions of slipping skin from the garlic, washing lettuce, and stirring a roux or risotto steady the mind, release imagination. I jot book notes on the backs of recipe cards — details, plot points, fragments of metaphors, images.

Gradually, a writing life reassembles itself within the form of this new life. When Janet arrives, I turn on the slow cooker, gather up a book bag, and walk to a café. There are new hours to spend, let loose in the imagination, hunched above a coffee mug, walking home in the late afternoon with new pages. The Miami sun is brassy, a razor burn on the back of the neck. A hundred familiar scents float in the shade, and I'm transported right back: childhood, little hamlet outside of Syracuse, climbing off the school bus into the smell of baking milkweed, pussy willow, Queen Anne's lace, the house filled with younger sisters and cousins waiting to be entertained.

Even when I was nine, conjuring up and describing to Aunt Aya my single life in airplanes above the cities and houses and sidewalks, I never pictured doing it alone: Someone in this dream-life always flew with me — a partner or friends. There would be an imaginary backdrop of parties, crowds next door. I wanted children — just beyond arm's reach — a sociable introvert's dilemma. Laziest of servants, I had only one entertainment to offer when I was a babysitter. After school and on the weekends, my younger sisters, cousins, and I were regulars at Flamingo Bowl. We wore the rented bowling shoes, creased by generations of children. Sprawled at our lane while Suzy kept score, Monica, Ibtissam, Dalia, and Farhad all rolled two-handed, slow-rolling strikes and spares. I brought composition notebooks along, slouched in the molded seats, drank root beer, dragged fries through lakes of ketchup, and wrote stories about escaping. The crashing waves of balls and pins and spilled sodas and pretzels all hovered at the edges, just beyond thought. I felt them around me, the small faces, the dark slices of their eyes, a nearby humming energy.

Who is the served and who is the servant? What I learn and relearn is they're inseparable, and frequently, quietly, they change places. The roles are unfixed, despite class, education, gender, despite anything. The one requires the other.

Janet takes home plastic containers almost every night, returns them empty. She requests dishes that I don't know how to make: ropa vieja, empanadas, and roasted pork chunks. I work on vanilla-scented flan, guava pastellitos, tres leches. One night, I hand her a cooling loaf of sweet Cuban bread. The next day, she tells me that they'd eaten it but I hadn't used the right flour. She gives me a cookbook, *Eat Caribbean*, saying, "I thought, since you like cooking, you might like to learn more." The book's edges are ruffled with Post-it notes: "These here are our favorites."

I spend the weekend cooking and paging through the book, trying to figure out the proportions for twelve servings. "Maybe I should just triple everything?"

"When did we open a restaurant?" Scott responds, peering into a bubbling pot.

One Monday, an hour after Janet's usual starting time, she sends a text: "Found new house. Moving to Pensacola. Sorry." Her cookbook lies on the kitchen counter.

That cobbled-together work life goes up in a whoosh. Scott is amazed. "How could she leave us? We paid her to nap on the couch and shop." I compose many different letters to her in my head in varying shades of pleading. Upset as I am about losing writing time, I'm more shaken by the sense of abandonment — it'd felt like Janet had grown into the shape of our lives. I find I miss waiting on her, miss picking up her plates and worrying about her family. We barely knew each other, yet we leaned on each other — weren't a lot of families like that? After Janet's departure, I begin to appreciate her labor a little more. Toys and picture books drift unmoored around the house. Scott and I start leaving crumb-filled plates in every room, creating our own fairy-tale path. Eventually, a couple of our worried neighbors send their daughter over, a teenager with a clear, intelligent gaze, a kind voice; she wears T-shirts and running shoes. She brings her own meals and rinses off her plates.

Writing comes back in the smallest dribs and drabs — sentence, paragraph. I'm careful, afraid these restored working hours will be yanked away like a magician's tablecloth. One word at a time, I reenter the manuscript. My process is attenuated but still in motion — increasing as Grace begins to sleep better. Scott takes over nights entirely and the work picks up.

One day, a new novel arrives at the house in big cartons, the cover a woman's face consumed by shadow. I take one off the top and stare at it, surprised it exists, this confirmation that it's possible to do more than one thing at a time. I open it and sign one for Janet, *Thank you for this.*

Janet got me started. That extra nudge that rolls the wheel.

Now, I sit outside at the café table with my notebook. I'll stay here and work until I can't see the ink. In the distance, bundled dark clouds move continents across the sky; far-off thunder murmurs in the ground, but up close a moth opens black wings, tumbling through the wind, playing, it seems, around the edges of the storm.

CHAPTER ELEVEN: PROTECTION

The look is a flick of light, fingertips of brightness on a crowded street, subtle yet a thing you can feel, the merest feather on the skin, as I walk with Scott and Gracie — a look absorbing the contrast of tan fingers interlaced with pale ones.

It's a familiar old sensation. I grew up with the look: It was there whenever I was out with Bud and his brothers, a bony thing carried along in a crowd of Arabic. Outside King David Restaurant, a man with a glittering afro and embroidered dashiki stood on the street with copies of the Nation of Islam newspaper, *Muhammad Speaks.* I ran to him. "My dad's Muslim!" I pealed. "Can I get one for him?"

The young man took me in: plaid sundress, peaked shoulder blades, swamp-green eyes, tumbleweed hair. He looked at the gang of skinny foreigners, arms covered in whorls of black hair, blocking the door of the restaurant, blasting their conversation. Back and forth he looked, then gave me a magnificent scowl. "No, little girl, I don't know nothing about that," he said, and huffed off to find a better corner.

The look is with me again today as we walk through the farmers' market. Here there are painters and poets, surfers and counterinsurgents, also men in hunting caps and boots, Union Jacks bolted to the backs of their pickups. There is the woman in the next booth at the St. Augustine Diner, complaining about the carved mahogany statue, because, she fretted, "St. Augustine wasn't brown."

If everything must have a color, then I call it lemon yellow. I feel the sour glance here and there, here and there, a tap, touch, game of hopscotch: I'm looking, no I'm not. I'd forgotten the stroller, so my baby is in my arms and I know it is generally a fine thing for people to look at babies. There are murmurs and doting smiles, admiring or sympathizing, from the people who remember what a ten-month-old weighs. We stroll past onions and berries and flowers and hula-hoops and kazoos. At a table covered with seashell night-lights, a woman folds arms across her plump bosom, resting them as if upon a tabletop. Her cheeks are pink and damp. She is watching us in that na-kedly hopeful way some vendors have, as though each browser represents the last pos-sibility of survival. Her wares are pretty if a little useless — how many scallop-shell night-lights could one person need? Still, I think Gracie may like to see this whelk light-ing up the hallway. Just after the moment of transaction, the woman places our seashell in a bag, bustles over change, and says to me, her voice full of Spanish moss and sweet tea on the porch, "Your baby is so pretty, and such an interesting color — was her daddy very dark?"

My own father has been idling at the other end of the table, touching and turning over every single item, bags of cucumbers and radish and pita loaves at his feet. He comes to lift Gracie out of my arms. Bud never said a thing about what any of his children looked like — nothing but beautiful, beauti-ful, night and day, *beautiful.* If you hear it enough, eventually it doesn't matter one damn bit what anyone else wants to say. I feel something inside me rearing on its hind legs and lifting claws — a raw, sudden rush of protection. I'm not usually this way. When curious, well-intentioned people ask, "Oh, where did she come from?" I don't always want to answer, "From the nation of none-of-your-business." Often, I will dutifully reply, "A little Puerto-Rican-African-Irish-Native-American-Arab. But basically Floridian." Just as, when people ask me, " 'Abu-Jaber'? Where'd you get *that*?" I don't always say, "Oh, I made it up." But today I don't like the way this one asked nor the set of her stubborn trout mouth. The woman watches me, Bud, Gracie, her face sharpened, trying to add up our colors. Perhaps it's not kind, but I say brightly, "Actually, I'm not sure who the daddy is."

On our way out, I hear Bud stop and say to the woman, his voice happy, very light, "You know what, the lemons are on a big sale, two tables down."

Once Gracie is walking, she wants to do it outside. Our house has no backyard, just a brick patio and a small pool. Out front there's a busy street with cars whizzing past. I'm continually aware of the effluvium of cars, their smell, their wretched, useless speed. Safety-hunting has become my hobby. Like a madwoman, I research communes and remote islands, places where cars aren't allowed. I try to hunt it down — that safe place. Where are the environmental laws stricter, the doctors better, the cars fewer, the stress levels lower? "There's this little community off the coast of Maine. You have to take a ferry. . . ." I read articles to Scott in the shared porch–office.

He nods slowly, rubs my shoulders. "Another idea — we could encase our child in a large Plexiglas egg."

I carry Gracie into the pool for the first time, an inner voice nagging me about chlorine and amoebas and when to start infant swim class. The water is warm as breath; she's laughing and agitated. Inside the house, the phone rings. Scott takes Gracie and I run, tracking wet footprints across the wooden floors.

"Ya Bah, it's your dad," he yells, his phone voice. "Well, I have not-bad news. Not so good, but not really bad."

My breath gathers in my throat. I'd half-forgotten, maybe on purpose, that we were waiting for the results of a bone-marrow biopsy. He's always been a champion napper, but lately he collapses into sleep. Black wings enfold and down he slides. I'd been dismissive, certain he was just worn out from moving to a new house — even if that was over a year ago now. Bud is seventy-four and full of heartiness. He has a tall, bullish build, good shoulders, a big round middle, strong bandy legs. Not quite seven months ago, we'd attended my father-in-law's memorial service.

"Well, okay, just so you know — I have it."

My uncle — Dad's beloved older brother, Hal — had recently passed away from a rare form of leukemia. When Hal was diagnosed two years earlier, he'd broken the news to us, boasting, "It's the best cancer to have." Supposedly slow-moving and treatable. Dad's oldest surviving brother, my Uncle Fred, was diagnosed with the same kind of leukemia nearly twenty years earlier and was still going strong. He took a marvelous pill that kept his disease in remission. But the great pill didn't work for Hal. After more tests, it turned out they had closely related, very slightly different forms of leukemia. Hal's was even rarer, harder to treat. And a third uncle, Jack, had died just a year before Hal, in the same ineluctable way — after an evening of parties and socializing: a hemorrhagic stroke, knocked down as if by a bolt of lightning. I try to take a real breath, but it's balled up in the center of my chest. I'm listening, but something pulses in my head. The day is spangled with pool water, the baby's chortling, the talcum-powdery-blue light over Miami.

"We weren't going to tell you." Bud keeps apologizing. He is lousy at keeping secrets

— the absolute worst. "I guess I thought you should know. Now forget about it. I'll be fine. I feel fine — tell your sisters, okay? Or, I'll tell them."

"Dad — what kind is it? What kind of leukemia?"

"Oh, I don't know. Something-something. Nobody gets this kind. That's all I know."

"Put Mom on, please?"

"Hon?" Mom says. "It's called chronic-something-something-leukemia."

"Chronic-something-something leuke-mia?" I try not to sound aggravated or terri-fied. If I'm not one way, I tip automatically into the other. I rub my eyes and they make dry little squeaks. There are sequins of pool water all over the place. My eyes ache with the brightness. Not now, I think. Not now. Not now.

"I'll find out," Mom is promising me. "I'll get back to you. It's long — the name of it. I'll find out."

A long terrible name. "Is it treatable? Is it the kind Hal had or the kind Fred has?"

"Maybe it is? I guess we don't know. It was a lot to try to take in — what the doc-tor was saying. We weren't really expecting to hear that. I don't know why." She pauses. "He hasn't been himself these days."

When I finally walk back outside, the pool

has changed. The water and sky seem to have shifted toward a fuller blue. Everything is somehow cooler and more beautiful, a taste on the tongue. Soft as cream and very, very far away. Light stars bounce on the water, bright as pennies, flung from their ridiculous distances. Into the air rises that sound of delighted, musical laughter.

Aggravation gives way to terror again. I'm no good at handling this level of anxiety. Dreams, clenched jaws in sleep, heart bounding, captured thing. The system floods with the need to run. Sleepless, I think of a morning years ago in Lincoln, Nebraska, when I was awakened by a blaze of noise. I'd stumbled out of bed to the blinds, dragging them open, and realized the bell-shaped objects mounted on the building across the street were some sort of siren. The sky seemed to invert itself, recalling the moment in sci-fi thrillers when the immense mother ship emerges from behind a cloud. The clouds themselves converged and there was a thunderous sound of wind. The top of the sky turned too white, then the white materialized into a loose column, a skyscraper. I watched the whiteness lean this way, then topple the other way, its narrow bottom telescoping toward earth, then, *zip!* The ground rose into a black veil, as though something had pinched up the earth. It lifted a black V and the whiteness turned black, and only then did I understand what I was looking at — the lazy conical tilt that terrified me as a child, every time I watched the *The Wizard of Oz.* An honest-to-god tornado.

My father rolls the fulcrum from terror to aggravation and back. None of us is brave. Unlike Dave, Bud finds nothing fascinating about his illness. His emotions roil the way they did when he was younger. He moons around their house, breathing complaint. Every time he stands, it's a theatrical event, an unearthly *ohhhh* from deep in his throat. Leukemia saps his strength, licks the marrow from his bones; his naps increase and intensify. Stirring coffee at the stove, he mutters under his breath. He grouses, unexcited by whatever diminished time is left to him. He and Mom have seen their friends obliterated by medical treatment. At dinner, he announces he wants to go now, go quickly. Done! Finish!

"I can't tell what's real and what's your father," Mom confides.

"End it now!" Bud shouts from the other room.

I want him to see a specialist, but Dad sticks with their local guy, "The Colonel," as we call him, a dour oncologist who seems to run the only clinic in town. His office happens to be close to a bakery, so appointments are bookended by cake and almond croissants.

Is this how it all ends, at a cut-rate body shop next to a Panera? At night I don't sleep so much as drift a few inches above the bed, caught in nets of fear and grief. In the morning, Gracie is there, sleeping sweat-suctioned to my arm. She'd climbed out of her crib and tottered to our bed. I try not to move. My breath rides on hers, a new form of calm. The raw early hour gives me a glimpse into normally guarded corners of thought. I risk stirring a few hairs off her forehead and consider how lucky it is that sometimes what you want is bigger than what scares you. Maybe desire is just its own kind of bravery. And you don't even have to feel brave if you can figure out how to just act like you are.

Other times, I'm at the computer into the deeps of the night. I hunt around medical websites for articles on Chronic Myelo-monocytic Leukemia — it has a name at last. Also known around the house as The Kind That Hal Had. But the resources available to the general public are slim: The only articles with any detailed information are limited to medical staff and other subscribers of stunningly expensive professional journals. Perhaps the AMA fears I might begin brewing home remedies in my kitchen alembic.

Reading and reading, I see names begin to reappear; over time, they become familiar as celebrities. Authors. Specialists. One name begins to glow — Dr. K, a department head at an august hospital, covered in honors. Just as important, his name is filled with Old Country vowels and syllables, a poem of a Middle Eastern name that Bud will love. I call Dr. K's office and am routed to some central clearinghouse where a clerk lies in wait, implacable as the Sphinx. There are forms and medical-history questions, a fortress of paperwork. The clerk says that in order to consult with Dr. K, you have to move to Texas, undergo a new battery of tests (including another of the dread marrow biopsies), and become a regular patient.

I hang up, chastened and frustrated. I resume online hunting: CMML. "This article restricted to subscribers of. . . ."

One night, I pull out the special name again. I have another idea — a slender message-in-bottle sort of thing. I peck around online and uncover an e-mail address. I write: "Please forgive me for crashing in on you. . . ." Maybe oh maybe the rarity of the disease and the reoccurrence in the family might make Dad's case more interesting. I describe his symptoms, his cultural background. I keep it short, under a page, sprinkled with apologies. I sigh and send, certain I'll never hear from this guy.

Minutes after sending it, an e-mail appears in my mailbox. Almost certainly some sort of automatically generated form — an out-of-office reply or a please-go-through-normal-channels auto-response.

It says, "Are you the novelist Diana Abu-Jaber?"

I read through a hazy shock: The doctor knows who I am. He's a big reader. He's reading my novel *Crescent* right now. He's read *The Language of Baklava* and he knows who Bud is, too. "How is that crazy, fantastic Bud?" he asks. "I want to know."

It feels like angels are laughing just over my head, shaking down stardust, at the good dumb luck of it.

Dr. K confers with the doctor in St. Augustine, studies Bud's charts and test results, then makes his recommendations. They have a kind of "targeted" therapy, with fewer pernicious side effects than those of the old-school approaches. The Colonel hands my parents a prescription. Within days, Bud has more vitality. His muttering simmers down and light comes back into his eyes. He splits his palms open, *tah-dah,* showing off health.

Dr. K also writes to me about books. He is a voracious, opinionated reader, his brain on hyperdrive. Every email is filled with titles he's reading in apparently every genre. An inhaler of fiction, he muses over nuances of style, character motivation, pacing. He calls my parents to check in and Bud trumpets into the phone that Dr. K must come to Florida for a social visit: "Come for a month. That's perfect. I'll make you grape leaves! I'll drive you everywhere! We'll go to the races! Do you like the races? We have a beautiful track, just gorgeous, beautiful. You come. You're a son to me. You're part of the family."

Bud wears himself out with the invitations. After the phone call, he moves us outdoors for the nightly gaze and talk — a ritual he started when they first moved to a place with warm nights. We're staying at my parents' beachside condo, where we can watch the pelicans drift in low formation over the surf. "There you are. Hello, buddies." He wags a loose hand at them. He points to a white planet over the black water. "See there. Who made that? I wonder. Do you wonder? Who made all these in the sky?" We study the night from our lawn chairs. "I hope I'm going to find out. I think I am."

His energy returns — once again he has a million stories, long yarns about sleeping in the fields among the family goats, about the lame midwife "Sitt Urjah," Limping Lady, who delivered him and his siblings at home in their village, Yahdoudeh, about the elderly man who taught them how to read while they sat in the shade of the lemon grove, the scent of sweet lemon mingled with aleph, baa, taa. Now he talks about the cloth sacks filled with powder they hooked over the children's shoulders. Powders from America and Great Britain, impressive chemicals. The children walked between the crop rows, scattering handfuls of silty white stuff on the plants.

"What was it, Dad?" I ask. "The white powder?"

He smiles and shakes his head. "Who knows? But all the locusts and field mice? They died. The Bedu wouldn't let their horses near it. Very good powders, very strong." He sniffs the seams of his palms. "Almost can smell it."

In America, CMML is a secondary cancer, a latent consequence of intense deliberate bombardment — chemo or radiation. Dr. K doesn't think there's a family predisposition but, more likely, a shared poison. Something the children got into their mouths or lungs. Now we know it came from America, sold to Jordan, along with outmoded antibiotics, canceled TV shows, unpopular processed foods. As Americans started jogging and drinking spring water, Marlboros became a national sport in Jordan. DDT — along with our other outlawed herbicides, pesticides, chemical agents — was a hit in the Middle East.

Yahdoudeh. So remote it could practically be a fairy tale. The desert, the animals, the fresh air, the stars beyond the stars: A child combs fingers through glittering white powder, pixie dust, and conjures the dream world of America.

Bud lumbers through the house and Gracie gives chase, screaming with laughter. He can't bear it if anyone scolds his baby girl or speaks to her sternly. He claps while she wiggles to his recordings of Middle Eastern music. If I tell her no and Scott tells her no, she runs to Jiddo. He sneaks her candy. Anything she wants. He tells us formally, repeatedly, "Her and me, we have a love contract."

He has given himself to her. He says, "I've lost my brains. The baby took them." He covers her head with kisses. "My queen, my love, my treasure."

Gracie accepts a few token bites from my plate, then inevitably slithers from her chair. She goes to Jiddo. Her favorite food is anything diverted at the last second from her grandfather's mouth to her own. She sidles next to him, contented, entertained, and eats morsels from his fingers, whatever he offers — tender lamb, stuffed grape leaves, tangy yogurt. If it comes from him, she'll eat it; we all notice this. Bud informs us that it's only natural. "She knows! She knows already, come to Jiddo for her food. Look at her. She loves family-style." There is a gentle permanence in the air; it glistens around them like air above the desert road.

"We're in the same wavelength," he says.

The three-year-old and the seventy-five-year-old hold hands at the table. Gracie commands, pointing. He gives her bites of lebaneh, falafel, grilled shish kabobs, stuffed grape leaves, hummus, grilled halloumi cheese. "She knows what food is. Just like Grandpa," he says, rolling the R in "Grandpa." Then he settles her on his lap, lets her watch all the cartoons she wants, and feeds her cookies. "We're the same," he whispers into her hair. If Bud gets up to chop, to cook, to help with dishes, she'll wait, then patiently take him by the hand and guide him back to the recliner in the living room.

"You sit der. Jiddo seat."

Bud has a good year on his treatment from Dr. K. His energy and blood levels go low, then bob and rise. We indulge in a period of hope: Just look at all the clinical trials, experimental cures, so many stories of breakthrough medical marvels. It's easy to lose yourself stalking through the Internet. This is how I pretend to be brave, trying to funnel all my thoughts into protection. Bud doesn't use computers. He reads the Qur'an in his room: You notice he does this more often than he used to. You all watch him now, even when you don't realize you are, minds split into two pieces, watching and not watching. He murmurs his prayers and watches the nightly stars, as if anticipating a message. Not too much changes. He doesn't abdicate, there's no slow retreat to the interior. He protects us by refusing to show fear — in whatever corners it might be crouching. He stays with us, fully himself.

After dinner especially, he's the same Bud as ever, sipping black coffee in the tiny cup, going over all the favorites — politics, Middle Eastern history, family gossip.

One night, sitting up in the living room, he tells me a story I hadn't heard before, about a betrayal, saying of a relative, "He could have helped me but he didn't. There was an opening, for the head of the king's diwan. He knew I would love this job, but he gives it to some idiot instead. Why does he do this? Because he can. That's why." He holds the cup pinched between two fingers. He's setting the record straight. It occurs to me, a low bell at the back of my mind, these are concluding comments, revelations of hidden old wounds. But then, the next evening, he says, "It's been a wonderful life. It really has." Passing my mother in the kitchen, he reaches out and startles her as he takes her hand, kissing it.

CHAPTER TWELVE:
WAITING, TRANSFIGURATION

First party: We hover around the crib, scarcely breathing in the dim light. Six or seven of us: People keep trickling in, holding fingers to their own lips instinctively, bending to peer through the bars. Before us, in the landscape of blankets, Gracie lies scrunched up, arms flung, face near-divine with sleep. Loveliness rises from her like a mist. Watching from the other side of the bars, inside our pooled breath, we could be something she is dreaming. At that instant, she opens her eyes. Her head lifts with a bright, startled look, bursting the dream with her smile.

Second party: The mixer purrs, whirling around the careful minutes. From her stool, Gracie watches closely. It's her first birthday and her first taste of chocolate. The room smells like a bloom of sugar and cocoa. Out of the oven, all day, the cake sings to her from its high place where we've tried to keep it hidden. She creeps into the kitchen, points at the top cupboard. "Ca," she informs me. At her party, she is briefly shocked by the singing and candles. High-chair-bound, she receives the first fascinating slice. She considers it for a long moment, then picks up a hunk. "Ca." She carefully nibbles. She stops suddenly, staring, motionless. Then all at once, all the cake is going into her mouth. Her face is covered in chocolate; she lifts fistfuls of cake; there are chunks in her hair. She grins fiercely, bares her teeth; she looks angrily awake, flabbergasted that this is the first she's known of such a thing. She is a sugar priestess. Her fist waves in the air, face thrown back, mouth open, as if to say *All chocolate is mine.*

Third party: Bring your kids! We were merry and casual about all of it and now there are twelve toddlers zooming around Gracie's room and swinging from the shutters. Various parents and older children filter in and out, trying to help with riot control, but a continual screeching, giggling, bashing, sobbing din issues from the room. It sounds like the primates house at the zoo. The adults stay in the other rooms with plates of bacon-wrapped dates, sliced torta, mascarpone on melon slices, shouting conversation over the racket. Occasionally, a shriek will puncture the air and one or another adult will put down a plate and run back. A few of the parents give one another pitying looks while the child-free people around them discuss movies.

As the night's machinery begins to wind down, the ones without kids yawn and stretch and decide to head home, and the ones with kids stay and stay, helping themselves to long, pleasant slugs of wine. Children begin to trickle out of their play space, small faces considering our adult rooms. They're wide awake in the amazing, frantic way of overtired kids. They chase each other through the living room, making a circuit, toddlers streaking and rumbling over the wood floors, around the coffee table, storming past the TV, smacking into the rear of the couch. We back out and look on from the dining room, clumped together as though on the banks of a river.

Somewhere in that gang are Belkys and Greg and Cordaro and Landa and Kai and Sandor and Madison and Tereza. But now it's just a tumult of kids. Watching them play, I remember a pre-child visit to Jamaica. I was standing on a silent beach looking at night-black water, its silver curl and ruffle in the moonlight. While I stood there, the pieces of moonlight seemed to rise into a cloud of enormous moths. They flickered before my face, bone-white in the dark, moon-flecked. I put out one hand to touch or part them and they drifted out of reach. Off they rose, crinkled gauze, leaving a larger, deeper darkness in their wake. I felt so sad, missing those night moths.

Soon the parents will put down their empty glasses, claim their children — one or two toddlers will outright refuse to leave; there will be hands pried from furniture, exhausted crying and goodnight kisses and backlit waves from the doorway. For now we watch them with pleasure. They are still running, thunder and shouting and that peculiar, pealing sort of laughter that comes just before tears.

Now time speeds; it glides through the eaves, I hear it everywhere, going so fast. I get an e-mail from Mom with the heading "Dad's Blood." His levels have started to fall again, misshapen white cells breaking apart. Bud's energy and spirits rise and fall with the number of platelets. I imagine the molecules of bone marrow like tiny cogs and wheels: Somewhere deep inside of him, a wheel has run off its track. Can't some tiny hammer tap it back into place?

Now the serious medicines are given through infusions, which sound a little like poisoned teas or flowers. Sulfur blooms spreading just beneath the breastbone. His iron levels are so low that his veins spring leaks. He can't contain his life force. Transfusions help for increasingly shorter periods; they don't catch. We rush back to St. Augustine to find Dad in the hospital again, face mottled with bruises, as if he'd been in a fistfight, the whites of his eyes eerily dark, like a horse's. Semiblinded from bleeds, his irises glow, hazel-brown negatives. Here is my father, umbrella to the rainy universe. My breath is thin; I can't seem to release it.

The medical staff has fallen in love with Bud. My parents' family physician, Dr. F., appears with lasagna heavy as a tray of bricks. "I told you!" he booms in the little room. "I made it! Didn't I tell you I would?"

"Mr. Big Talk. I didn't believe you. Shows to go me," Bud said — getting it sideways. The way I thought, as a child, everyone said it. "Shows to go me."

When it's time to release him, nurses line up in the hall beside the requisite wheelchair. One kisses his hand, the other the top of his head. "Here they are, my girls. Let me count them. Beautiful flowers. Come here." He widens his broken eyes. "I can see my flowers."

The floor nurse takes my hand. "Your dad. Good lord."

Mom and I marvel at it: What does he do in there? He just talks. He calls everyone sweetheart and tells them he loves them and talks and talks and never stops. The usual.

Gracie drapes herself across his lap and chest, fills his face with her cloud of hair as she watches TV. She expects respectful silence during cartoons and shushes the room, her hand resting on top of Jiddo's, a diadem.

Beyond the sliding glass doors, there's a broad swath of green. My folks live in a new development. Out front, the house shows its clean, spare face to matching neighbors, but the back of their house faces a large round pond bustling with egrets. Bud coaxes them like cats onto the lawn. There's also an orchard, a rock streaming water, stepping stones, tangerines, olives, kumquats, rosemary bushes, live oaks. Bud shows where he'd put in trellised grapevines. Over time, their backyard has turned into a Mediterranean garden. Rustling with perfume, the yard contains mosaics, tiled tables, umbrellas, terracotta planters, clay figurines, torches, chimes, dark laughter, glass ornaments — caprices — in the high old branches of the pines. The Isle of Capri behind a modular home in St. Augustine. Every year, my parents line the palmettos with so many Christmas lights that we see cars line up to roll past, Bing Crosby melting from their windows.

Formerly the most-requested Muslim Santa Claus of children's wards across Syracuse, now in civilian-wear, Bud gazes out at the colored lights. These days, getting up from his chair requires rolling forward, nearly toppling out, hands braced on knees, shaking, groaning, pushing, trembling upright. He still brews, then carries a nightly demitasse of *ahweh* on a saucer across the living room; we all watch the quaking porcelain. His medications give him tremors, gusts of hot flashes. His people have assembled for the holidays and no matter how we yell at him to relax, Bud has to make us dinner. He sits at the table with his blood-burnt eyes, assembling a pot of stuffed grape leaves, elbows out, fingers curved around the slow, precise rolling. The pinch of filling, just so, at the center of the leaf. Just this much olive oil, that much tomato. "They're getting cheap, these guys." He shakes the emptied glass jar. "I counted the leaves. California leaves, they're the best. Used to be forty-two. Every time. Now it's thirty-six. They think I don't notice. These guys. It's the sons. The father would have a fit." He can see well enough. The rolled leaves are trim and taut. He puts in the peeled garlic, a whole head. "That's the good stuff. Right there."

A bite of food, a story over the plate, this art is ephemeral. Bud's brother Hal — who'd grown angry and then angrier still over his illness, had said, "What a shame that I have to die, what a loss, with all that I've known and seen and thought!"

Working at the table, deeply meditative in this fluid, unfixed thing of cooking, making his art, Bud is contented.

Scott hoists the brimming pot to the stove for my father; down it goes with a clank. Bud says, "I don't care what anyone else says about Scotty — he's a good guy." His go-to joke. He will try it on waiters, flight attendants, bus drivers. Sometimes people get it.

"Oh, I don't care what they all say about you — I think you're a great guy!"

"I'm not afraid of death," Bud tells me. "I'm just afraid of doctors."

The days orbit appointments: urologist, GP, oncologist, home health nurse. In between, his cronies come to badger him into poker, betting on the ponies, political debate. Occasionally a visitor will want to make everyone bow their heads and pray. "That's okaaay," Bud assures me, Mom, anyone in the room. "I don't mind. Who should I mind? I don't care. I need extra. Jesus, Muhammad, the Easter Bunny, Buddha. Who prays the loudest, that's who I'm standing next to."

After the holidays, despite all his predictions, Bud is still alive. Most of the visitors have gone, and Scott, Gracie, and I are due to return to Miami tomorrow. Bud proposes dinner out. "Let's go to somewhere," he says. "I'm done cooking." We pull into the busy lot: Not quite 5:00 p.m., and already a line of people winds out the restaurant door. Bud says, "Never mind, never mind — go on in. You'll see."

We can barely squeeze in the door. The hostess must have looked past the crowded lobby and noticed the antsy three-year-old, the elderly gentleman with the bruised eyes, and his post-holidays exhausted wife, because, magically, there is no wait. We're ushered to a table. As she passes out menus, Bud beams at the woman. "I don't care what they all say about you — you're a great kid. You're A-one in my book."

Dad can't see well enough to read the menu, but he never reads it anyway. He gives the server a million special instructions. Lifting his palms, making rays with his fingers as if about to reveal the most amazing secret, he tells the young woman he'd like a "good steak." Plenty of salt and pepper. "And don't be shy about the butter. A good salad on the side with sliced radishes, cucumbers, herbs, don't forget, and nice olive oil and lemon." When it arrives, Gracie climbs out of her chair and stands next to him, a hand on his arm, cadging bites. He kisses the back of her head. "She's fluffy but she's no dope." Bud watches us and the other diners, drinking in their voices. His steak has a good salty crust and a melting swipe of butter. "There, they did it," he says, still surprised when Americans get the food right. The room is filled with sliding black lights, currents of laughter; there is something aqueous, submerged, about the place. The light has a winking quality: It seems we're on a boat together on a dark night. Where are we going? The beautiful black waves glitter, time filled with quiet distance.

Back home, once again we stay up late

talking, lounging on the couches. Late night settles into the ligaments of the house, insects murmur in the windows. In the midst of casual discussion of all things, Bud tips back in his chair, saying again, "Such a wonderful life. So wonderful." Outside, there's the ragged line of pelicans, making their hajj, the shadow flight, low and tantalizing above waves — but we're not at the beach — it's odd to see them this far inland, their forms like flakes of black against the dark.

In the morning, Bud feels good, his energy up. Scott, Gracie, and I are headed back to Miami in a few hours, but first I'll drive my parents to Bud's weekly checkup. He kisses his granddaughter at the door. "I love you, *habibti,* my darling."

"I love you too, Jiddo."

He stoops to kiss her round hand. "I love you."

"You already said that."

He laughs and slaps the top of his head. "The queen is always right."

At the clinic, he heads out of the waiting area to visit with a row of chemo patients pinned to their easy chairs. In the examining room, he tells his oncologist, "I don't care what anyone says about you, you're okaay." There's just one thing, one faint scratch on the fine day — a numbness in his hand and leg that the doctor squints at, frowning. Finally, he sends us to the imaging center for a scan. Bud is already thinking about lunch, asking for "maybe just a little soup. Go to that bakery — they have cake." He signs a release form as we wait for the scan. After the attendant takes it, Mom touches my arm and whispers, "Did you see that? He couldn't write his name?" I shake my head, willing it away — his vision is off and today for some reason his fingers are funny. "Something's not right," she insists.

Bud touches my cheek as I sit beside him trying to test his vision, holding up my hand. "What do you see, Dad? How many fingers?" I'm trying to be brave and present, to muster a few atoms of strength, protecting myself from this thing that I refuse to notice. His voice is round and tender and he smiles at me, a look like sunlight angled over the earth, "There you are. I see you." He kisses my fingers. Like that, I'm four years old again, and he is telling me what is important to see.

As we wait for his results, there's another surprise: My parents' good friends Moira and Connell Duffy appear. Bud's pals are all getting scanned and X-rayed these days.

Connell has lived in the States maybe sixty years, yet he still has a good, strong brogue. Bud has leaned against Connell's shoulder many times, communing on the extraordinary experience of finding themselves here, fellow immigrants in a land of barbarians. Now Connell plonks down beside Bud and slaps his knee. "Fancy meeting you here."

Connell, with his shock of white hair, tips against Bud; they look ready for a hand of poker. I want to keep thinking that things are compromised but normal, that Bud will struggle on and on, this broken-down-ness our new normal. Oh I see the woozy tilt, but I don't see it. I want to tell Connell, somehow, that things aren't normal at all, something is wrong, but I don't know how to say it. I can only sit here, watching the men. Mom rises, the enormity of everything quietly dawning around us. "We need someone. Now." She rushes off to find a nurse, her footsteps sharp cracks down the corridor.

Bud can't believe the luck of this encounter. "When we going to Ireland?" he demands, his voice thick. "I want to go." The words slur between his teeth.

"This summer! Let's go." Connell's face is thoughtful. "We'll go to Dublin, man."

"What's there to see there?"

265

"All kinds of things — pubs and pubs and Trinity College."

"What's there? The college?" Bud's voice is dissolving. I can barely understand his questions. I stare, unable to work out what's happening. Connell manages to hear Bud better than I can. He says, "All sorts of things, art, and poetry. They have the Book of Kells."

Bud wants to know more. He says something we ask him to repeat. I can just make out, ". . . Book of Kells?"

"Ochh." Connell rolls back in a way I recognize — the contented talker. The *charming kind,* as Gram would've said, followed by, *watch out.* "It's quite amazing, this very old book — a sort of mystical book — with fine writing, and such illustrations, my man, like you've never seen."

There's a thin, soft light in Bud's eyes. I think he's distracted, seeing the gold-leaf filigree, the swooping calligraphy of his own holy book. The books of his mother's library spilling open, words fluttering out like snowfall. The book is the thing. We lean together, our mutual languages encircling us, binding us in their traces. There is just enough time for the three of us to imagine and agree on this. Language lifts her pale hand over our heads, the words growing fainter and older: English, Gaelic, Arabic, as all around us the air grows bright, nearly blinding.

CHAPTER THIRTEEN:
WHAT LASTS

Who says? I want to ask. Who made up this terrible way of doing things, where we are given these people, people that we need, we absolutely require, and then whoosh, off they go? Nothing lasts forever? *Oh yeah, says who?*

Hospitals are either very good or very bad at handling certain foundational realities, depending on how you look at it. Their corridors are tunnels between worlds, their people are guides, pointing to different doors. Florida medical facilities are especially weird, cool and dry inside, with big windows bounding with light and humid colors and bending palm trees — all just beyond the glass. That's where I look, mind emptied into that sheer light, as if there was a way for us to run away from this place, skip off to distant blue islands, just as Mom returns with a tumult of emergency nurses and EMTs. An ambulance pulls up right outside the door. We're in such a distant wing of this complex that they will drive him to the Emergency Room entrance. It seems Bud's scan shows a brain hemorrhage — white moth wings of blood, the angel in the brain, ready to wrap him up. A nurse comes to my father, takes his hand, half-kneeling on the floor, I think she's explaining what is happening to him. I'm listening, but everything is so close up and sparkling, so sheer and blue — I don't know what to pay attention to.

The ambulance doors explode open, its interior crammed with men and equipment. As they load him onto the stretcher, Mom and I try to tell Dad we're coming right behind him, we're on our way. Everything has been shocked into high speed. I pull Mom toward the car — we must follow! We reenter the corridor, charging toward the parking lot and there is her friend Moira — they are talking wildly, hands on each other's arms, clinging to each other. Mom breaks into tears, saying, "His brothers — this is how it happened."

At the front of the ER entrance is a young woman with light brown skin and forest-green eyes. She shows us to a quiet back room, speaking to us gently, part counselor and part ambassador. Minutes later, two doctors come in. One is Bud's oncologist, his face pink, hair scattered, as though he literally ran here from his clinic, across the oceans of parking lots. He points to a page in a folder. "Gus has a living will?"

No, yes, but wait. Wait. Wait. At some moment, very soon now, all this twirling will stop, I think. There will be a quiet space and things will stop. The blood will calm. We'll put Bud in the car and take him home with his bad eyes, and now he will have this angel in his brain. It will just be another thing. I stare at the cranial scan on the wall before us. We can live with this.

I must have said something, I don't know what, because the doctor shakes his head. "We might prolong his life a little bit with machines, but. . . ."

Mom nods, firm and pale. "No — that's how he wants it. No heroic measures." My throat tightens. I hear a whisking, flapping in the air, something too close. I will reach into the air at any moment now and make it stop, I think. Because this can't be. This is not how it happens. People don't just sit down in a room and decide they can let go of each other. I refuse to make that decision, and any second now I will say so. I will say, *Just wait.* And yet here I am, nodding with Mom, as if we are agreeing, though my eyes stay cool and dry and I am filled with disbelief.

The ER doctor leads us into Bud's area, a big, dim room made of curtains. We take up vigil beside his bed, one of us on each side. Mom and I each hold a hand. The EMT driver apologizes — they sedated Bud in order to intubate him. "We didn't realize he had a living will," the man admits. "We wouldn't have done it." Now my father floats just beyond us in a state of twilight unconsciousness, his breath a ragged snore, so our last words take place through this veil of anesthesia. The doctor encourages us to talk to him, and somehow Bud does seem to be listening. I squeeze his hand. "Don't be afraid, Dad," I say, because I'm so scared and I don't know the right thing to say, but I can't bear to think of him feeling the way I'm feeling right now. "We're here," I hear myself saying. "We'll always be together. All of us." We stroke his head. Time speeds up, slows down, paced by the rhythms of his hard breath and the hospital monitors. We call my sisters, one by one, and hold the phone to his ear so they can speak to him as well. His breathing quiets as their voices trickle into his ear. He's listening. After each call, Bud nods, several times. He'd waited to hear from his children.

Only then does his heart begin to slow.

Several of his nurses from past hospital stays get word that Dad is downstairs. They join us, hands clasped, to bestow their last kisses. The young ER representative who first greeted us, our guide, with her narrow, caramel-colored fingers, soft hazel eyes, errant hair — a wisp of a creature with a fairy's face — sits a while, telling us about herself. She loves to work with the critically ill, people balancing on slim thresholds. She uses the words *potent* and *profound.* At one point in the conversation, I find I'm touching her hand, as if trying to tether her, like a balloon on a string. I'm not quite sure she exists.

Despite the cascade of bleeding, Bud hangs on. All his life, my father had been so physically strong; now, despite his winnowed blood, his organs struggle to keep going. Nothing in him wants to let us go. We wait, hold as still as possible, watching him do the work of it, inch by inch and breath by breath, the blip on the monitors growing fainter. Labor. Gravity loosening its hold. Later it will occur to me how lucky a good death is. Completion, the transformation into wonder: to feel beige walls melt into plains of clouds, to watch faces turning, glittering. Though he is leaving, I have the undeniable sense that he is going somewhere, tunneling through the air, in motion. We watch the monitor. There is one last blip. The last sweet drop. His spirit rushes over the palms of our hands.

The nurse stands by the bed, watching; seconds later, she says one soft, "Okay." She marks the time, leaves quietly.

Mom stands to kiss the top of Dad's head and she tells him that she's happy for him. He's wanted to go for some time, we know. Then she sits beside him again. After a moment, she says plaintively, "I don't want to leave him all alone here."

"Let's stay." I haven't let go of his hand. "We'll stay for as long as we want." We sit with him quietly, companionably, his spirit so radiantly present it seems to me nearly as if nothing has happened. This is a sense that will remain with me for weeks after his death. I'm not given to mystical beliefs, but now I'm struck by the ordinariness of it all, expecting perhaps a great gash in the air, yet it seems somehow quite clear that he hasn't gone anywhere. Even now, perhaps ten minutes after the last solitary heartbeat, it feels just as if Bud is still squeezing my hand. I wonder if on her side of the bed Mom can also feel the press of his hand. When finally I let go, his fingers open slowly.

■ ■ ■ ■

We are pulling the car out of the hospital parking lot when Mom says, "Oh no. Oh my goodness, we forgot Dad's clothes — in there. We've got to go back."

We could probably reclaim them another day. In fact, we don't actually need them any longer. But I swing the car around. We pull up to the curb, and when I reenter, a nurse says they'll bring his things out to me. A few minutes later, I see her through the window — our guide with the fairy face. The young patient rep comes through the door with my father's possessions in a plastic hospital bag. I'd held off tears all this time, but as she folds me in a hug, they rise, as if embedded in the skin. She tells me, "There's people in there crying that —" She has a wide, helpless smile. "It's not usual. Nurses and doctors coming over, telling about him —" She shakes her head. "I'm so sorry I never met him."

I can hear him now: *I don't care what they say about you — you're a great kid.* I can't help my own shaky smile. "They did — they broke the mold." I thank her again and think to ask her name. She tucks a few strands behind her ear and says, "I'm

Grace."

At home: tables jammed with salads and casseroles and pies and fruit displays and flowers and shrubs. The doorbell, the house phone, the cell. A tribunal of old men in the living room, Bud's rickety, bony-kneed cronies, their faces wide and dazed or closed, grief-confirmed, into seams. In the dining room, Mom finds herself consoling distraught plumbers and landscapers and handymen. People Bud had routinely bargained down. They keep looking around as if expecting him to emerge. Wanting him back. He's been gone for several hours and that's enough.

"My wife didn't even want me to work here anymore," the electrician says forlornly, bent over a cup of coffee. Mom pats his arm as he mutters, "I was losing money, working for Gus." The man holds out his hand, palm up, weighing something. "He made me nuts. The way he'd stand over you, telling you how to do stuff he had no idea how to do. And his jokes? Oh, my God. Those crappy jokes."

A houseful of weeping men recount incomprehensible jokes. "Remember 'worse than guilty'?" the landscaper asks. They mutter and shake their heads.

Bud's terrible gag: "One day, the king decides to make a challenge. He says he will give his finest stallion to anyone who can come up with a 'crime worse than guilty.' " If you're in Bud's audience, now you say, "But what does that even *mean* — worse than guilty?" He doesn't have a good answer to this. "So, the king's joker, Jeha the fool, waits until the night of a big party. When the king and queen are in the receiving line, Jeha comes up and pinches the queen's bottom. The queen shrieks and drops her champagne and her crown falls off. The king shouts, 'How dare you? Take this dog out and shoot him!' And Jeha says, 'But Your Majesty, first you owe me a stallion.' 'How think you this, you evil, you monster?' And the joker said, 'You said a crime worse than guilty, did you not?' And the king had to admit he was right, and that was how the king lost his best horse."

That's it. That's the whole joke. If you're an American, this is when you frown. If you speak Arabic, you might also frown. But you might also eventually say, "Ohhhhh!" Then translate it into Arabic for your friends. They will have a good laugh. But not the English speakers. Unless it's a night like tonight, where the joke gets told and mulled over, and no one gets it, but they can't stop trying.

That evening, Mom, Scott, Gracie, and I take a drive to get out of the house. "Where is Jiddo?" Gracie asks for the third or fourth time as I sit beside her in the backseat. I feel the hairline crack in my chest as I say, "He's gone, Sweetheart. He's not with us now."

"When I can see him?" She watches me struggle, confounded, trying to offer her something. "I don't know, Baby. Someday, I think."

Through the tall pines, there's an immense, glittering sunset. It soaks the moving car, lights everything with gauze, flames the branches into white shadows. "I think the sun wants to come with me," she says. Squinting at the radiance, Gracie strains against her car seat and points. "He's over there! I see him! Hello, Jiddo, I'm right here. Hello. Hello."

CHAPTER FOURTEEN:
THE RIGHT THING

There are many parts to the walk to preschool.

The elevator, in which you are the only one allowed to press the buttons.

The lobby with the doors and the first shock of whatever the weather is doing.

The walking up the hill with many backward glances — has the streetcar already come, is it coming yet? If it's rolling up to the stop as you straggle down the front steps, there are two long (uphill) blocks that have to be run, hearts banging, school supplies, hats. Much backward yelling: Come *on,* Mama! Thundering through its doors just in time. Which is all pretty silly, since it's usually faster to walk to school than to ride the streetcar. There are seating arrangements to consider: sit beside Mama, in the seat behind or in front, and if Daddy's there, where does he get put. There are many faces to look at and to see what sorts of things are people wearing and are they appealing or not. Is there someone interesting aboard, perhaps someone talking loudly to someone who isn't there, or someone who smells like no baths, someone who merits special attention?

After the trolley are more blocks, also a raised embankment of jagged stones that Daddy calls "hot lava," where Mama says, "I don't care if you're sort of holding her hand, it's still not safe." And you have to run across screaming so the boiling lava doesn't burn through your rain boots.

Half the time or more, it's raining. When you get to the school, it's old and pretty and covered in ivy and it smells, Mama says, like a real schoolhouse. There are stairs and construction paper and cubbies. The world shrunk down to its best size: The big place out there is too big and this is the size things are meant to be.

It's almost the bad part. Not quite yet. First there's a little story in the reading nook with Mama. Then hang coat on low hook. Then say hi to everyone standing around. Then three hugs and four kisses or thereabouts. Five kisses, twenty-three hugs. This is the *plan,* which got invented when you woke up on the second day and stretched out in bed and picked up Big Dog and said, I'm not going to school today. Maybe next week. And then at school when Mama said goodbye and gave kisses and went out so quickly, you were laughing because you could run down the stairs and get to the front door even before she could. You could do it three times in a row! And then Bella the teacher asked Mama, What do you want to do? And Mama said. . . . And Bella said, I can hold her. Say goodbye and I'll hold her — this happens a lot in the beginning. And Mama's eyes looked big and sad shadows were there, and you wanted her to say, no, maybe next week. But instead Mama said, Well, she's really strong.

And Bella said, I'm strong too.

Three kisses and four hugs because there is love here and work over there and we stand between the two places, love and work. If we do this just exactly right and do it the same every time, maybe it will soften the scorch just a bit, the coming-apart to discover our new worlds.

So I let go and see you smile and start to launch yourself, to race down the stairs to the front door, but Bella grabs you with both arms and lifts you off your feet. I see her face register the shock wave of your body, your remarkable strength: Is it physical or is it your will, root-deep, like your scream, a curtain of shattering glass beads, the wild-horse eyes you train on me as you thrash and shriek: "MAMA, DON'T LEAVE ME."

You don't stop. Your voice rampages behind me: I flee like a coward, though someone else (another parent?) is also in the hallway shouting (humorously?), "Courage!" Your voice is there on the staircase, in the hallway, at the front door. "MAMA, COME BACK. MAMA, MAMA." It doesn't stop until I'm outside the building, on the street, the sounds of traffic swarming over my head, my heart trying to fly out of my throat. It's all I can do not to turn and run back up those stairs.

But I don't because the teachers said this was the best thing to do, the only thing to do, that if I give in to your demands, it will never get easier. Because I have to teach my own classes and go to meetings, and there is no other option. Because friends have told us there is nothing better for children than a school and this is such a good school, so progressive and sweet. Because we're trying to learn each other's lessons: to demand and to release. And two minutes after I've started walking, legs shaking, toward our home, Bella will text a photo of you laughing, building an enormous buttressed complex of Legos with some other children. "She's fine. She calmed right down after you left."

And it does get easier after that: You almost start to enjoy school. We settle into routines. Yet I still regret that day, all these years later. I don't know if I will ever stop regretting it.

A magnificent day of sunshine, a friend's house vibrating with feet and voices. The party is too crowded and too loud and threaded with hyper kids. Regrets and shadows and backward glances are dashed out the windows with a sorcerer's broom. How do you put a life into perspective? Maybe you have to invite everyone over and ask them to tell it, ask them to hold up memories like tiles in a mosaic — step back and see what pictures emerge.

People have flown here from everywhere. Bud moved so much that someone observes, "The mountains have come to Muhammad." People holding highball glasses lean against the front wall to tell weepy anecdotes about Bud's tenderness and his short fuse, his cheerful madman hospitality and his lousy tips. His willingness to stop everything and talk to anybody at any time. His pleasure in a good, top-volume fight. His unbelievably bad financial advice. The time he invited an airplane full of passengers over to his house for dinner. His stuffed grape leaves. His shish kabobs. His jokes. His indecipherable political views. His breakfasts. The time he sat at dinner with a group of lefties deploring the war in the Persian Gulf and announced his hopes that America would "blast Saddam Hussein off the planet." The time he wandered away from a tour group in Hawaii for half a day to follow "the voice of the earth." The time after the hurricane, when he and Mom set up a food line outside their condo and cooked breakfast for thirty-seven neighbors. Finally, Connell Duffy makes his way to the front of the room. He's slow and deliberate, and when he gets there, he props himself straight-armed on a sturdy chair back. "Gus used to tell me, 'You know, you and me — we're different from these others.' " He nods, his handsome Irish face startled by grief, tousled white hair falling forward. Bud understood him, their homesickness one of their great, shared experiences. "He was right, you know. That Gus. Gus knew. . . ." His voice wobbles. He has to sit down before he can tell us. What did Gus know?

■ ■ ■

After the tributes are over, my husband calls
for a toast.

We had to comb St. Augustine to find the
araq. The licorice booze, so sharp and hot,
Bud's ritual celebration drink, crucial as his
nightly shot of coffee. Derived from aniseed,
araq has medicinal uses — for stomach-
aches, to lighten the heart, and to improve
storytelling. One can marinate chicken in it
or make a lovely geranium liqueur or an
incendiary sangria. My father liked to sip it
before dinner, an aperitif with some mezza
— a few nuts and chopped vegetables. I
grew up with the understanding that a few
bites and a few sips, either in conversation
or in quiet meditation, were a marker of a
civilized life.

Here's a story that I don't tell at the
memorial. Years before I was born, when
my father was just a teenager, my grandfather Saleh lay dying of stomach cancer.
Bud cooked his meals and then quietly
soaked them with araq to help dull the pain.
My grandfather (according to Bud) had
always preferred Bud's cooking; eventually
Saleh sent away everyone else. "I was the
only one who could stand his screaming,"

Dad would say, rubbing his temples to soften the memory. Sighing at his cutting board, as if regret and uncertainty could be pressed with the tines of a fork, ingredients soft and cool as butter. "There was so much pain. Day and night, screaming and screaming." When Bud was a child, his father's drinking was such that Bud used to help his mother hide the araq; years later, when his father was dying, Bud returned to all the hiding places and unearthed the bottles. My father had cooked and soaked and served, and withstood the screaming. What I learned from that story was that sometimes, even when something is very hard, there still isn't a better way to do it. You might mourn something and still do it that way all over again.

My brother-in-law, Don, assembles the drink in the traditional order: pour into a short cocktail glass one part araq, then two parts water, then some ice. Make sure you always assemble it in this order or the oils from the araq will separate into a film and condense inside the glass. Araq means "sweat" in Arabic. Some say this condensation is where the name came from, but possibly it's a nod to the drink's sly potency: Once you add water, it's milky white but strong as sin, unlocking desire, the scent of black licorice on parted lips.

My other brother-in-law, Lance, carries a tray around the room, handing out diminutive cups. The room buzzes with interest, inhaling the vapors from the milky drink. There's a pause in the conversation as we touch our dainty glasses then knock back the shot. It pools, a pearly liquid silence.

It occurs to me, maybe we should've warned everyone about araq.

The gasp is like a jet door thrown open. One hundred proof — some brands even stronger — the drink has a demure anise scent and a donkey kick. People grab the arms of their chairs, one of Dad's cronies pops up and then falls back in his seat, a woman claps both hands on top of her head. Someone says, "HO MAMA."

Huffing, wheezing sounds roll through our memorial service. A gray-haired woman in the back of the room is already rolling forward on the couch for another. Araq is its own lesson: It hurts you and makes you want more, like so many things, like falling in love, like loving anyone so much that you can never imagine that you won't have them forever and ever. And the life continued on the other side of that person is like nothing so much as a dim, gray mist. And this is what Bud knew, even if Connell didn't say

it out loud: You regret not a bit, not any of
it.

Chapter Fifteen:
Work and Recovery

At my desk, a glaze of computer light in the late afternoon, I can hear dinner sounds, soft tick of pots and spoons and husband's and daughter's voices. I feel ghostly, eavesdropping on daily life from this point of remove, as if I waited on just the other side of a membrane.

Here is the writing life, pure observation, yet I chafe against it as I listen to them laughing. Here is work; I must work. Still, their voices pull at long strands and tendons. I want to get up and go out to them. I need to work a while longer. Work is what saves you. For a few minutes, my concentration returns to the page, then they break back through. I take in the scent of frying onion and garlic, my daughter demanding crayons, ice, wrestling. There is her voice asking, Where's Mama? Though she knows. My fingers hover, held midair above the keyboard. I lower them. She keeps closer tabs now, having recently learned that someone can leave the house in the morning and not return in the evening.

I thumb through a few yellowed pages of *Dubliners,* searching. The voices recede as printed words sift through me. I'm on an Irish city street in a snowfall, the flakes brushing my face, my body feeling buoyant and distant. *It was falling on every part of the dark central plain, on the treeless hills, falling softly upon the Bog of Allen and, farther westward, softly falling into the dark mutinous Shannon waves.* There is a rustling sound and Gracie stands between my knees. "Mommy," she whispers near my ear, "can I tell you something?" She steps on my feet, climbs onto my lap. "I want to write words. On the work." She points at the computer.

"You do, do you?" I hold her so close I can't see the screen.

"Write 'Gracie' there."

"Here, let's write it on this paper."

"No, there. There. On the work." She knows that's the thing.

"How about over here . . . ?"

"No! Computer."

We write GRACIE in capital letters in the middle of the sentence in the middle of the page. She checks each letter, studies the total effect. She says, "That's better," before running out.

"Mama." Gracie is clutching my arm, her voice compressed and urgent. She's just dashed back from inside the house. "You come with me *right now.* There's something. *In there!*"

We're still in the driveway, unloading suitcases after the six-hour drive to St. Augustine. But my daughter is a passionate, frequently undeterrable person. The week before, she'd awakened us before dawn in a storm of tears, wailing, "Where is my tiara?"

I stop everything to follow my three-year-old. She runs into the guest room and gives a full-armed flourish like a hostess on a game show. There's a new painting on the wall over the bed, its colors bending and swerving, a pointillist cascade. Mom follows us in to see our reaction.

"When did you buy this?" I ask.

"Well." She laughs softly, glances at the carpet. "It's really weird. I just sat down the other morning and this painting just sort of came. . . ." She twirls a hand in the air. "Spilling out."

About twelve years ago, my mother took an acrylics painting class. She produced a series of vivid beachscapes and portraits. Bud gazed upon these wordlessly at first, filled with a kind of fretful pride. He said things like "Look what Mom made!" She painted for an hour or two each afternoon at the dining-room table, then removed her work each night in time for dinner. We bought her supplies and canvases, but eventually Mom stowed it all away. "Your father doesn't like messes. And painting is pretty much mostly messes. It just takes up so much room." She shrugged.

Now Gracie stands on the bed, sweeping her fingers near the canvas in a swoon. She returns to this post several times over the next few days and I have to offer her distractions — cartoons, vanilla pudding, an extra bedtime story — to get her to leave the painting alone.

That new painting is just the beginning. Gradually, my mother's house fills with images of water and movement; her brushes litter the dining-room table. The place where Dad used to sit rolling grape leaves is where Mom now leans over an easel, the tablecloth stiff with smears of burnt sienna, royal blue, cadmium, and titanium white. Her new work is electric, bolder than the pieces she'd done years earlier. The walls are covered with canvases, windows filled with half-faces, figures swimming through clouds and air and flowers and words. At seventy-three, after a half-century of Bud's stories and opinions, my mother steps into the new stillness and starts to work. I wonder whether my grandmother Grace — herself filled with barely suppressed energy — had sensed this desire inside her daughter, lying in wait. "Women will pour everything they have into a man," she'd lamented. Mom had quieted her artistic self, Bud had acceded to living in the States: Was this what each of them had given up for the other?

Even though Bud was big-mouthed and overbearing and generally seemed twice as large as he really was, my sisters and I lived in the space that he and Mom made between them. Without Dad, we shifted, looking to see what would fill the empty place. Who was our family now?

"It's the most beautiful," Gracie says, sprawled backward on the bed, gazing up at Mom's painting.

"What do you think it is?"

"A sea witch?" she asks hopefully, though there's no discernible human shape on the canvas.

I contemplate the work, its expansive, dotted, brilliant motion. At first I'd thought the painting depicted my mother's freedom — released from caretaking and my father's ailments, released from fifty-plus years of marriage to Mr. Personality. But later, when I remembered how she'd bent over his bed after he'd passed away, kissed him, and said, I'm so happy for you — you're free, I think it's the shape of my father's light as well.

Drive straight north, out of Florida, and just keep going. Our rented cabin is perched on the lip of a small Adirondack cove overlooking a cobalt lake. We sleep well in this place: It might be because of the air — thin, pure, clear, and cold. Dusted with pine needles, traces of old smoke. The fresh, feathery air echoes that of my childhood — not far from here. I keep listening for Bud's voice, certain he's just around the corner. This could be the summer when I was seven years old, in bed before the sun went down, drowsing to the sound of my parents' voices. Though I've never been to this little community before, there is the delicious sense of return. Already we have small familiarities and routines. Early to sleep, windows open, then, seconds later it seems, a voice crosses my dreams: *Hello? Hello?*

This is a fluid time, just after Bud's death, a boundary-waters place. I want to carry on as usual, do my work, talk to people, but it's like combing fingers through fog. Work goes, conversation, concentration. Some of our friends already seem to know about the gray time — they call us with invitations, lures out of the normal world to possible retreats and sanctuaries. One day I say, Sure, let's go.

Here is a terrace and railing from which you can view the blue distance. My three-and-a-half-year-old daughter has discovered she can climb out of bed at first light, cling to the railing, and yell greetings into the valley. Then, wondrously, one or another of the vacationers in the cabins inside this grassy bowl will look up from their coffee (or their beds) and call back.

"Good morning, Gracie."

"Hi!" cries the child. "Hello, hello!"

"Yes, hello."

"GRACIE." Scott is sitting up in bed. "Get back in here."

There's no way to stop her or close her in; nothing locks. The door to our bedroom is a sort of glorified shower curtain; there's no door at all on her room. Early riser, she evades us each morning, waking me with the same dream, a tiny voice floating out of the clouds.

Our meals in this easy place are delicious. Hamburgers on the grill, macaroni and cheese, cold fried chicken and salad. All day, kids play on the swings and slide or swim in the cold lake, the air hot and dry. By evening, everyone is ravenous. One morning, we drive into Vermont to pick blueberries. Gracie devours half the berries before there's time to stir them into muffins, her lips and palms stained blue for the rest of the day.

We stroll back and forth to our friends' cabins and present ourselves by peering through the windows, then wandering in. Privacy is pretty much nonexistent, but no one seems to miss it. The adults agree: This is the way we should live! No television or computers or gadgets! Good food, clean air, exercise: reading on the terrace until last light. The children bask in this sudden swath of freedom. No adults saying, "Oh, no no. Don't go out there. Hold my hand." It reminds me of the early days, when you were able to roam all day on bicycle, riding through new worlds filled with other children.

Divisions and boundaries begin to ease — not only the walls but also the lines between the home and outdoors, between the family and the gang. Our families flow into each other. Gracie runs around the valley with the older kids while we look on from grown-up distance, our lawn chairs and grill. When Gracie shouts in the morning, it must feel to her like she's gained a magical power — the ability to summon greetings and voices from unexpected places. A sense that the world might be closer and sweeter than she'd ever realized. It's a fuller life, a village life, not so different from that of my father's Bedouin clans, for whom parenting was general and shared. This, it seems, is the tribal existence that Bud was always trying to return to. I feel guilt-pricked, thinking how I never understood what he wanted, how impatient I was with his dreams.

Eventually, though, it rains and the children are cooped up and cranky. At bedtime, Gracie vows she's wide awake, she'll never be sleepy again. The air turns biting in the morning; we recall our old lives and start to miss them. Soon we'll be returning to houses. Soon, I suspect, I'll start to feel grief.

On our last morning, I stumble out of bed, trying once more to intercept her, but there it is, with the first streaks of pink, the voice shouting, "Hello? Hello?" Five or six people call back. Most of our valley is awake. One of the two sisters who own this property confided the other day that they'd nicknamed Gracie "the alarm clock." Resigned, I join her on the terrace. She leans on the railing as we watch the morning embankment of fog sparkling over the water. Erased by mist, the loon lifts its voice, so mournful I feel a shiver between my shoulder blades. "Good morning!" Gracie hollers.

"Honey, too loud."

The bird calls again — long, unearthly notes — as if it were summoning souls back to the earth. An improbable new member of the family. Gracie says, "Mama, I have to tell him. He's waiting."

How lucky it is, once in a while, to be able to hold still. The fog shimmers in place, a tiny pocket, a gap in time's fabric. Later, it will burn away over our car, our dazed thoughts trained on the highway, a hot little cinder starting in my center. Now it's only us and our faraway bird — these greetings called, tossed out, our voices connecting in these invisible places.

Chapter Sixteen:
Want

She's lying sideways on the chair, head and feet hanging. She wants us to feed her this way. We tell her to sit up; she does briefly, then slithers, knees first, to the floor. "I wan eat down here. This my underhouse," she says from beneath our legs. "I'm a puppy-snake. I ate your feet." Now she wants us to throw "scraps" to her the way she saw a woman on a farm tossing orange peels to a rescued pig. She licks our ankles, then bites them. I yell, "GRACIE." Scott gives me a long, she's-your-daughter stare across the table. Really, it's just another version of the new-parent conversation we have these days: Are all kids supposed to be this hard?

People say to us: It's girls. Boys are so easy — they're puppies. Girls are difficult. They always want something.

Girls need things to be happy, my grandmother told me crisply. Dolls, dresses, all sorts of stuff. She puffed her cheeks, overwhelmed by the futility of it all. She couldn't afford it, but she couldn't help herself. She bought us things (though we learned to be careful and not make requests), then said, "If you leave your new clothes on the floor I'll haunt you after I'm dead."

Now my daughter lies flat on her back on the floor, breathing heavily through her nose for some reason. "Pretend I'm canni-ball" — a word gleaned from some wildly inappropriate cartoon. "You gonna eat my pieces."

"Baby. *Up.*" I feel around for her unsuccessfully, unwilling to get on my knees.

From somewhere under the table: "In two minutes."

"Baby." I'm talking to under-the-table, but I look at Scott, sag, imagine my grandmother laughing. See how it is? Didn't I tell you? "Come up. Don't you want some dinner?"

Why won't she eat? We ask each other. What does she want? The question taunts us. She won't stay at her plate: maybe three bites, no more. What is the secret food or flavor, the token, the word, the gift that will hold her, lure her out of the underhouse? I lower the fork under the table and she nibbles at it. I feed her nearly a whole plate of food this way. The more they don't want to eat, the more you want to feed them. The more difficult they are, the more you love them.

No, I'm fine, I tell people. Oh, I feel a little kicked in, burnt around the edges. Singed. But otherwise fine.

The stream of Bud's voice really has stopped: a stream that had run so continuously, I don't notice it until it's gone. I sing lullabies to Gracie before bed, drawn toward the sad-sweet songs. There are so many pointed edges now, snags, unexpected grief-traps hidden here and there. I see a fat gourd of a vegetable at the market, unidentifiable, and suddenly feel tears, realizing Bud would know how to cook that. I gravitate to certain friends — cooks and immigrants. When a favorite chef moves back to France, I call him to say goodbye; afterward, I sit down, feeling something like the heel of a palm press against my chest, thinking of his round Mediterranean eyes.

But really, I'm all right. I'm looking for a house.

I wake up one morning seized by the idea. So *that* is what I want. A talon closes around me and it becomes all I can think about: *We must move.* Solid and new, the idea of a house — of looking for one — clears me out, smooths away edges. I will think about nothing but this.

Scott and I had talked about getting a bigger place for years, but only recreationally. There were just the two of us when we bought our Miami house — a glorified studio. Good old floors and sly whimsies — a paw print in the floor of the enclosed porch, inside shutters, carved archways — but minuscule. We have to open the shower door to sit on the privy, the floorboards shriek and crackle, fumes from the garage wisp directly into our shared office-porch. One lively morning, the knob comes loose from Gracie's door, shutting her inside with me until Scott unlocks it with a butter knife. When we get out, I say, That's it. Buying a better house strikes me as the embodiment of growing up, making space for a family.

I spent half my childhood in the backseat, Bud driving in tireless circles, Bedouins wandering the deserts of suburbia. Hunters. For years it was the thing we talked about: where to live, where? Bud in the car, arm out the window, fingers drumming against the metal, worry beads swinging side to side from the mirror. Houses lined up like soldiers or reclining like odalisques, gazing back at us through the windows, taunting: Maybe your true life is here. No, wait, maybe here. We moved so many times between my first grade and the start of high school that teachers asked if my father was in the military. I couldn't explain. "What about that house? Look at that place." Whenever we pulled back into our driveway, Mom — trying to tether us to something — said, "Oh, look. Who lives in this sweet house?" The children cried, "We do, we do!" Bud remained silent at the wheel. The problem wasn't the neighborhood, it was the whole country. He couldn't fix that part, couldn't settle in. After she finally left her parents' home, Grace moved just a few blocks away, to live in the same small apartment for more than thirty years. She said, "You get one house and one church, one country, and you stick. None of this dancing around all the time."

He tried to move us back to Jordan, but whenever we got there, it seemed to hurt him just as much as America did — not being the place he remembered and longed for. Oh, it was lovely, but the night no longer shone with lilac streaks, the air was no longer spangled with stars of bitter almond. No more beautiful parents or family cosmos. Some of those things were there, just not the way he remembered them — which was even worse.

Bud taught us: any house might hold a magic portal. All you do is find the right one. Stare hard at those front doors and windows until some inkling comes to you, a sense that here, this is home. Each house has its own language. A micronation. You're choosing not just a home and a neighborhood but an identity. Find the structure, settle in, as naturally as a soul dwells in its body. What was the grail after all, but a tiny home for blood and spirit. And who doesn't want to find that?

"Look at him go, go, go," Gram commented, watching Bud pull out of the driveway to "go looking." "Lord only knows where he thinks he's headed."

Scott and I can't afford a bigger mortgage, so we tell Travis, our new realtor, that he must perform a magic trick and find us a bigger place for the same amount of money. We start searching within a mile radius of our house, but each neighborhood lazes into a new one, with so many enticements — nice lawn, second story, bricked driveway, wide sidewalks. We drive into corners of our town we never knew existed. Travis's car is soft as amnesia, a small continent of air-conditioning and black upholstery. In here, it doesn't matter that something terrible has recently happened. Grief has a backward gaze. No wonder Bud adored house-hunting — it was a kind of antithesis to sadness, all forward momentum.

Each weekend, back into the car I go, sinking into the shadowy interior, drifting farther and farther afield. Travis hands us color printouts — prices and school districts. We travel farther north, squinting as the square footage increases and prices inch up. It is fine, all-consuming, Sisyphean work.

Each time the door clips shut, I settle into the seat, something murmuring *forget, forget,* behind my ear.

On a day of sterling sunlight, we pull into a driveway. It's forty-five minutes to the north, just a few minutes from the condo where my parents used to live. I look out, palm on the car door handle, and hesitate. The place looks small, slightly scrunched, hobbity. Still, when the car opens, I smell salt water in the air. The beach is a few blocks away; it ignites the sky, the windows in the house flare. "You can walk to water from here." Travis lifts a hand, his eyes broadsided by light. The palms that circle the house wave and undulate, and sunlight seems to wag through the air like brilliance thrown off ocean waves. We enter through an aquamarine front door, and the rooms flow from one to the next, filled with this particular sunshine, everything ocean-colored — the walls, the paintings. A sea house.

The owner hurries before us, throwing doors open, going room to room, pointing out tiles behind the kitchen sink, a lamp of colored-glass fruits twinkling over the dining-room table. She studies me with stark eyes, talks through every detail, complains about other prospective buyers. "People are crazy! They're all, 'Oh, the ceiling is low,' 'Oh, the rooms are so small,' 'Oh, why is the clothes dryer in the kitchen?' Can't they *see*?" She fans out her arms like Maria in *The Sound of Music,* marveling at her house, at the insanity of the world, before the listing agent comes in and steers her away.

Behind the house, in the center of the little backyard, my sister and I drop into the grass under a tree's dense canopy. It's like something grown out of a fairy tale: fat, emerald leaves, half-wild, the crooked trunk all burls and knobby roots. "I better get up now," Monica says, staring at the clear blue sky, "or I'll never leave."

I glance back at the house and notice the owner watching from the door.

■ ■ ■

Travis is in the kitchen going over numbers on a clipboard. He reveals, with a lowered glance, that this sea house is priced far above our already-unrealistic top price. I laugh and say, Forget it, though my breath constricts with disappointment. But he's shaking his head. He grew up on a working ranch before becoming a real estate agent, and when we met I recognized my father's wily old horse-trader gene in him. "This house is way overpriced," he murmurs, an eye on the door behind me. "It's undersized and pretty oddball — the layout is kind of kooky. And that weird blue front door?" He gives me a look like a poke in the ribs. "I can run comps for the area. She could drop it a fair bit before things start to line up."

I think about her hot eyes, the swoop of her arms. "I don't know, Trav."

He reclines against the countertops. "Y'ask me, it's been listed for four months. It's getting tired. And the way things are going — in this market?" He lifts an eyebrow. For the first time in years, housing prices have dropped. Travis regularly hands us stacks of printouts of newly sold houses in the areas we like: Nearly every sale has shown a plummet in asking price. Like Bud, our realtor likes the edge of a counteroffer, playing with that fine line between insult and possibility.

In the second bedroom, the owner swirls up behind me again, talking as though we were in midconversation, delivering stream-of-consciousness family history. Her father built the place seventy years ago. She and her husband remodeled it themselves, top to bottom — see that sea-glass backsplash? See the porthole in the bathroom? Eight years of remodeling. They were finally done; they were going to travel. But her husband dropped dead four months ago. Bad ticker. She was all set to retire this fall, but now she isn't sure what to do. Maybe cruise around the world? Maybe live in a van by the river with her dog? Like a hobo! Ha! Ha! Ha!

"Okay there," the listing agent enters, stealthy as a nurse. She puts a hand on the owner's elbow. "I was just wondering where you'd gotten off to."

Thoughts of the house circle me during the ride home — the glass tiles on the bathroom floor, the color of the ceiling. I can't shake it — the doorbell, the name of the street, the way two yellow Adirondack chairs face the front lawn. A more sober piece of me can see, yes, it's patched up and only half-repaired in places, the roof appears to be crumbling off the walls, and we plain can't afford it. But the house inhabits me. It's as if, with the story of her husband's death, the owner draped a gauze over the building, its details watercolored by loss: I see their hands on each cornice and railing, imagine the way she and her husband moved through their home together. The place is burnished, polished by grief. Enchantment falls over me. Some piece of my hidden sadness has come forward to join hers, key in a lock. It turns and opens a door in me.

The price unnerves him, but Scott admits he likes the rambly yard and clean garage. After months of looking, it's a place we finally agree on. We make an offer — tens of thousands of dollars under the asking price. It's still more than we can realistically manage, yet it feels like dropping a penny into a wishing well. I tell myself I'm ready to be disappointed, but I've learned from watching my father that bargaining is as much about having faith as anything else.

We wait to hear back. I stare at the phone; I live with it in my hand. Occasionally I turn it off and on. There are five endless days of silence before the listing agent returns with a counteroffer that is almost the original asking price. Beside the barely adjusted amount, in capital letters are the words FINAL OFFER.

"So that's that." Scott rubs the back of his neck. "It was worth a shot."

A knot of disappointment forms in my throat. I chew on my lips, thinking hard. "But still, she came down," I say. "Not enough, but still — maybe that's a sign."

"What? Like a secret message? She's making her counteroffer in code?"

I jam my hands in my pockets, scowl out the windows. I'd seen Bud wrest unbelievable deals from people — merely by smiling and refusing to let up. He called it *us'meh*, but he willed it into being. He haggled in supermarkets, movie theatres, and shopping malls. He haggled with car mechanics, telemarketers, and Girl Scouts (then he tipped them). He haggled with the turnpike toll collectors. He got his price.

Travis agrees with Scott but he also talks strategy. "Let's just let it cool off for now. Give her a little time to stew in her juices. And it can't hurt to keep looking, right?"

But I see us in that house: Gracie a schoolgirl, fishing from the backyard dock, a preteen getting burgers at the corner store, in high school, walking a dog down the sandy blocks, working out algebra equations under a rainbow-striped umbrella. Such a house, some tiny, crazy part of me thinks, dispels sadness. I try to give *us'meh* a nudge and write a note to the owner that I hope sounds less desperate than I feel: "I wanted to let you know how much we love your place. I understand what a special place it is to you and how much history you have invested in it. We would be honored to be able to add to that history."

Only later do I realize how little that letter is about the house.

The new pages look pale, almost watery in the dark morning. Four a.m. I am writing instead of sleeping, a penlight hazing over the notebook.

This book is ineffable and elusive. At first, I thought it was going to be the follow-up to my memoir, another book of family stories and dishes. But for some reason I keep describing it in different ways: I tell a few friends it will be called "A Food of One's Own." I tell a bookstore audience that it's going to be a feminist manifesto — with recipes! Other days, I think it will be about how to raise a good eater. If only I knew how to do that.

Though I'm staring at pages, at the back

of my head, I'm listening. There is a chamber in me that is absolutely quiet, still waiting for my father's voice. After my grandmother's death, I continued to have frank conversations with her — generally while in the kitchen, standing by the mixer or the oven. A whiff of nutmeg, rum, and chocolate from an open cookie tin and she appeared, leaning against the refrigerator, scolding me for not setting the timer, or airing her philosophies of love and relationships, or filling me in on the necessary components of a young woman's education.

Where is my father's ghost? While he was alive, there was nothing more maddening, endless, and impractical than Bud's advice. Now, of course, I miss it — oh, I miss it.

Concentration whisks away, words dissolving, sugar in tea. I get up and drift through the house to my anchorage. We keep the night-light in the kitchen. I take out my soldiers — flour, brown sugar, vanilla, salt — wisps of powder like magical capes. I don't know what I'm making until I'm into it, sighing and stirring. Tonight an apple crisp; tomorrow, caramel bars; the next day, angel food. Here is the last sanctuary: The cool, methodical steps will clear the air, the recipes soothe me with their calm voices, and the sugar brushes away sorrow.

■ ■ ■ ■

It seems that evasions and denials belong to the grown-up world. My three-year-old wants unsoftened answers.

"Where is Jiddo?" Gracie asks each night before bed. "I can see him?"

I make stuffed-animal voices, dance her slippers around on my hands, sing "Puff, the Magic Dragon," stalling for time. But she asks again, "Where he go?"

"Well, he's gone, Sweetheart. For now. Jiddo died."

"Where is died?"

"I don't know, Sweetheart," I say in a kind of surrender. "I wish I did. No one really knows."

"About died? No one?"

"Not really."

She thinks about this, her solemn eyes resting on mine, trying to imagine there might be something that not anyone knows. "Not even Daddy?"

I stroke her curls back. "Not even."

I think this will be the beginning of a difficult metaphysical discussion; instead, she says, "Can I have some gum now?" She sinks onto the pillow beside me, arms tucked beneath her head. For this moment, we lie still, side by side on the bed, gazing through a transparent ceiling, into stars upon stars. Children know you have to live inside worlds of questions — only the adults forget and think they have to make up answers. Who made you, I want to ask those stars.

I send Travis back to offer another five thousand on the house, though he resists at first, warning gently that it isn't going to work and the house isn't worth it in any case. When that's turned down flat a few days later, I storm around, something inside of me stabbing away. I stand in the kitchen by the loud fridge, glaring over the counter, which opens, for some reason, into our shared office-porch. "That could be *our* house now! Why doesn't she know that?" I'm joke-shouting — only most people probably couldn't tell just from listening to me.

Scott squints at some online story about sharks and surfers. "Unless she wants her asking price."

"She's torturing me!"

"Yes, she's torturing you." Scott smiles at me. "Or another way of looking at it is she's being direct. She told us what her price was, and she's sticking to it. Unlike some people."

Is it obvious how this will go? How Bud's house fever grabs me, simmering up, how I will send Travis back again and again, to make small, additional offers that eventually approach the full asking price. A series of mad offers and refusals. Yet, while I'm in it, I don't let myself look at what's happening. Unraveling. I can't stop wishing. It isn't the house I love — it's the sadness. I even understand why the owner isn't selling — she can no more let go of grief than I can.

I lower myself into the chair, scrape it forward, rub my fingertips over the thin gold sovereign that hangs around my neck — a memento from Bud. My memoir lies dormant and half-abandoned in its far corner. I open the file and try to find my place again, start writing. Stop. Decide I can tell this story without mentioning Bud's death — just skip right on over it. It's my book, goddamn it, and if I say so, he never has to die at all.

I type and cut and rewrite and give up. Go into the kitchen. Return with a slice of cardamom cake. Turn my chair firmly toward the computer screen. It's like peering into a fun-house mirror: words and images and thoughts and memories emerge on the page, but never in the way you expect. You imagine the story you will write — it feels as effortless as gliding on ice — but then you begin and the words turn dense and cumbersome and it's like hacking through a forest with a butter knife.

It's always been like this for me, but now it's even worse. The words sink back into the foliage, wild and scattering. There's a large, shadowy figure in the forest. It shimmers darkly, bearlike, impossible to make out. I keep trying to look past it. Silently, it rises on two feet. I watch, my breath catching, trying to think how to write this. I cannot write this. I go back to the kitchen for more cake.

New listings. Travis points out big windows, roomy neighborhoods, full, glimmering branches. He wonders, very quietly, if perhaps I wasn't more taken with the interior design of the sea house than the actual house? He talks to me as softly as a grief counselor. I go forth, peer into refrigerators, closets, bathrooms, distracted by the details of people's lives — their books, the shoes neatened, heel to heel, beside the bed. Each new address is a deep breath, plunging under, water snapping in my ears. It's been weeks since we've traded offers and rejections, and I tell myself I've let go of the other house. That other place.

We drive out to view a house in the far-flung beach town up north. I realize the sea house is in the vicinity but don't know exactly where. Gracie is with us, laughing away, bounding through the rooms while I run after her, hoping the listing agent will think that I have things under control. "Sweetheart, do not get on that bed." I stop in one room, swept by déjà vu, and realize dizzily that I can view the sea house through the back window.

Gracie comes in the room and grabs my hand. "Why your face look like that?"

I pick her up in both arms — she's heavy — and bounce her a few times. "Oh, I don't know, Baby."

She laughs, throws up her arms, and expertly slithers from my grasp. Travis leans in the entry; his smile draws lines in his face. Gracie flings her arms around his knees, nearly knocks him down, then runs from the room. Later today, he and his partner, Marco, will be trailering some horses to Ocala to sell. Unsentimental about horses or real estate, he has a direct, business-first approach to life. He'd told me recently, "Get the value lined up, the love can follow." Bud would've been crazy about him, I think. Then I'm pierced by a sudden awareness of loss. I sit on a desk chair and exhale, pushing against sharpness. I turn away to squint at the corner of that window. "Somebody's full of beans today," I say.

"So, hey, will you look at that?" He glances at the sea house through the back window, then perches on the edge of the bed across from me, clasping his hands loosely. "Funny thing. You'll never guess what I just heard. The owner's taking that house off the market."

I stare at him, unsurprised, yet a cold little eddy of rage snaps inside me. "After all that time and back and forth. And we offered her price. Just what she wanted."

He shakes his head. "Didn't want to let go of it. Could be she figures she'll get more money if she waits and relists it in the fall."

"She can *do* that? Just — say *no,* just like that?"

"She did." He leans forward, tapping my knee. "Hey? You okay?"

I'm thinking about saying something about how we couldn't afford the place, it was too small anyway, there wasn't a crawl space or a yard or enough room to sit up in bed, how it's really for the best. I know that we'd just made a narrow escape from an

317

unpayable mortgage. Mostly, though, I'm just observing my own emotions with some curiosity. Once my anger passed, the house fades like a puff of smoke.

Travis crosses his arms and settles back, unusually pensive. He sighs as though someone has told him something confounding. "You just don't know what folks are up to in this business sometimes. I mean, look, people don't like a lot of philosophy mixed with their real estate, but I gotta say this. I see crazy stuff happen and I end up feeling like that's fate — you know, what happened with that house. Seriously. I think that one wasn't meant to be. All the other stuff aside, comps and value and design — somehow it wasn't going to be your house." He shrugs lightly, the sun shearing through his blond razor cut.

As I consider this familiar old sentiment, I feel another pulse of grief — the realization that some day we will find a place to buy, that we won't be able to keep spending every weekend with Travis, letting him drive us around like a ministering angel. I say, "My dad would've wanted to know why you aren't married."

He smiles. "Because that kind of marriage isn't legal yet in Florida."

I turn my back on the window and follow

our realtor out the door. Once more I stop to take in the salt air. There's one of those big, complicated Florida skies, layered with clouds and light, palm trees twisting and reaching in the distance like retirees in a calisthenics class. A line of pelicans drifts above the rooftops, blown in from somewhere. They hang for a moment, pinned there. *Hello, buddies.* A dark new form. Just one more shadow in the world.

I feel loss prickling all over, the coolness left behind on the skin when something beloved goes, the sense of immense strangeness and possibility. So many ways to write the grief story, through tears or dreams or memories. Or houses or cakes. Losing my father is, for a while, like losing my home in the world. The soul's seat. No house on earth brings that back. A hundred thousand ways to avoid grief — and each of these ways, it turns out, is a kind of grieving. Sorrow comes, transmuted or not, water through the barricades.

For that afternoon, at least, I decide I don't need a house. I'll make my home in the trees and grass. Sit on the sand with a notebook. When the pelicans come to call, their ragged necklace laid out against the sky, we'll examine each other, earth to air. You'll find me writing this story, telling it

all, gazing back at you as you skim past,
barely moving, watching.

CHAPTER SEVENTEEN:
POWERS

Almost-four-year-old Audrey has long, tapering fingers, a haughty neck, slender arms designed for pushing away dishes. "No," she says. "No. No. I don't eat those thing. I don't like those thing."

Almost-four-year-old Gracie sits close beside her friend at the picnic table, narrow legs dangling, watching intently, her face filled with pleasure at this beautiful new world of refusal. When I put out slices of cheddar cheese, a bowl of salty olives, some smoky chorizo — items my daughter loved a week ago — she announces, "I don't like!"

It seems as if humans are born into their best, wisest selves, without fears or biases, unaware of age or skin color, indifferent to beauty or deformity, ready to absorb languages, full of curiosity and adventure. But how quickly all that vastness and possibility begin to fall away. We'd heard the tales of children who would eat only white foods, or liquids, or single ingredients — "air ferns," one friend calls them. We'd seen these kids at the table, faces drawn up tightly, a withering eye cast upon their plate. Generally speaking, if we don't make a production of things, if we don't assume Gracie will turn up her nose at the radish, the aioli, the sour pickles, she will take nibbles. If not a bite, she will lick it; if not a lick, then a sniff. There's a series of pictures of Gracie at one and a half lounging on the kitchen floor eating a slice of lemon: She bites it, then winces, incredulous, then bites again. The tasting-and-wincing goes on in several frames: When I try to dispose of the chewed-up lemon, she breaks into tears.

Bud ate the whole lemon, rind and all, biting right in as if it were a peach. He taught my sisters and me to eat the seeds, the white orange pith, the crispy chicken skin, the marrow from bones. He remembered what it meant when food wasn't taken for granted. He was descended from a family of noble cooks and big eaters. We joked that the Abu-Jaber family crest should have a picture of a rearing locust.

Grace and Audrey chase each other around the picnic table, ignoring the food, their cries streaking the air. A week later, my daughter will forget to refuse and once again nibble the olives. But the crusts of toast will go untouched, the tomatoes will be pulled out of the sandwich, the orange segments will be sucked down to wilted little cases and left for dead. I joke ruefully that I'm going to start an organization that will feed the whole world — the Kid-Rejected Food Bank. Then I spend an extra twenty minutes removing even the thinnest pips from the cucumber, without needing to be asked, because I know — she won't eat the seeds.

The doctor wheels the stool up close, her cool blue eyes intent on mine, and says, "Tell the truth: What did you eat today?"

My gaze loosens up: I travel mentally to our Formica and particle board kitchen with the curling floor tiles, think of pouring batter into the waffle iron. Gracie hanging onto my leg. It began nearly the moment she was ready for solid food, the pancakes and waffles, the banana breads, the baguettes and encrusted scones, pull-apart biscuits, the brownies. We stir, gazing into the bowl, inhaling whiffs of cinnamon and vanilla. Gracie's compact body hums with an audible pleasure. There's no fast food, but there is this steady daily procession of baked goods. And, I admit to my unsmiling doctor, not many vegetables.

Her brow is tipped forward in her hand; I see the dismay of someone who's heard it all yet continues to hope. "Your blood pressure, your blood pressure," she murmurs. "I can put you on medications or. . . ."

"Or?" My paper jacket crinkles as I stir on the table, a blip in my voice.

"You can lose a few pounds and stop eating all that sugar."

The chill of the office seeps under my paper garb; my feet go cold. "Oh. Uh." My hands snake around my middle. "Do I have to?"

I consider Lenore a friend, forward-thinking and restrained — her medical advice is usually doled out in thoughtful measures. "A little sugar is one thing — but a lot?" Her pale irises fix on mine. "It hammers you. Your body can't handle the overload. You get inflammation and insulin problems. Weight gain is the least of it. There's a cascade — elevated blood pressure means hardening of the arteries means heart disease." She trails off, intimating dismal ends.

But I don't know *how* to lose weight, I tell her, almost begging, feeling useless and wimpy. I literally cannot imagine not eating sugar. Our new house has a fine oven made for baking. And since Bud's death, I've had trouble finding my way back to dinner: It doesn't taste quite the way it's supposed to anymore. The ancient war between Bud and Gram, dinner and dessert, has lost its balance. No more waking up from a nap to the scent of onions, lamb, and okra — Bud's tender *mia bamia* stew, filled with tomato and garlic. Such moments were rare in grown-up life but still possible — the lure of waking into warm scents, anticipating the meal cooked by someone who loved you. Now, instead of cooking, I pull out a few quick bites of this and that for our dinner, then bake a chocolate tart and hand-whip a bowl of cream on the side.

Years ago, my grandmother's death had taken me, like a guide, into grief, and then led me safely back out of it again. Now I lean on her ghost — the one she'd promised would haunt my messy room — for consolation.

There were times when my grandmother's baking was the greatest good — witching hours when the colored crystals and grain of the dough were indistinguishable from brushstrokes. Which is part of sugar's hold on me — such big pleasure, not only dessert but fairy dust. On the last morning of our trip to Paris, years ago, before my grandmother and I were to catch our flight home, one lonely pastry remained uneaten. A fluted cream puff preserved in the sort of clear clamshell box that florists used for corsages. I'd held it up to the light, peering into the box, examining the scroll of petals.

I understood Grace's passion for baking, her art. Like painting or singing, pastry seems to transcend usefulness. The opposite of nutritious, people call it "decadence." Or "sin." Dessert is lovely because it's transgressive. It exists for pleasure, for itself — echoing Grace's instructions throughout my childhood: Create your own meaning. Wait for no one.

I'd wanted to take that frosted orchid back to America and keep it forever, but Grace had said no. "It won't be good if you wait. Eat it now or forever hold your peace, dahlin." In the hotel room, on the side of the bed, my grandmother and I cut into the cake with a knife borrowed from room service. We ate the crisp scrolls with our fingers, inhaling oranges and sweet cream, closing our eyes.

Lenore gives me a scrap of paper with a name and a date on it. A great speaker, she says. This will help motivate you.

I am chastened, mind-numbed, bones

buzzing as I walk out of the office, recalling the mournful set of Lenore's mouth, the way she shook her head over my test results, as if refusing them. Cholesterol, blood sugar, blood pressure: no, no, no. "Don't you want to set an example for your daughter?" she had asked. I will change, I vow under my breath. I lower my head, repentant. I will change my ways. Vegetables, I murmur, a supplication. Vegetables, vegetables. And no more sugar. Even if offering something sweet out of an oven feels almost exactly like doling out love.

Grace was the fountainhead, the wellspring of sweetness in the world. She'd lived through the Great Depression, raised a daughter on her own, worked without respite for years. She knew the importance of a little sugar in life. It was her mission to make sure that her granddaughters never went without.

Her apartment had a crawl space in the ceiling. It opened with a neat ladder that folded up like a trick. Up the ladder went Gram, her plump hips visible as her upper half disappeared into the ceiling. She brought forth armloads of candy. In an apparently perfect union of form and function, she poured her granddaughters shot glasses of M&Ms. So easy to eat, so pleasingly crushed between molars. They were so small and so many and so colorful, it seemed you could lose entire days sprawled before her grand old TV in its cabinet, crunching, crunching.

Whenever she visited, her first order of business was to "run out for some staples." Grace loaded a few granddaughters into a cart and wandered the aisles, picking up a loaf of bread and carton of milk before veering to the candy aisle, where she told us to pick anything. A moment of such freedom it was almost psychedelic. The cart filled: licorice whips, butterscotches, and nonpareils. We grew uninhibited and threw in all sorts of exotics — candy dots on paper, redhot dollars, orange marshmallow "circus peanuts," chocolate cigarettes wrapped in candy bands.

"Gracious." She admired the bubble-gum cigars. "How cunning. What won't they think of?"

"This is so cool, Gram. Mom and Dad never let us do this." Bud was suspicious of sugar and loved to claim he never ate "white food." The pleasure of the palate, for him, was all salty, bready, meaty, cucumbers and yogurt and olives. But that wasn't the whole truth. He was often forking into a cake or pie while bragging that he didn't eat sugar. When we were a young family, each night he brought home a chocolate bar and broke it into five pieces: one for each of us.

My grandmother would place a quart of Whoppers in the cart, murmuring, "I know how you love these."

As we shopped, Gram treated us to a running critique of our father. "Oh, he thinks he's high-and-mighty. So typical. He thinks he runs everything. Well, just let the Great Dictator stop me now." Gram said exactly whatever you weren't supposed to say. She said it like she didn't even have to think about it first. Like she couldn't even imagine not saying it. And this daring and this freedom was mixed up with the sugar, as if they all went together. We were a family of women, sugar fiends, shameless and unbowed.

A few days later, I sit in an audience, each of us with notebooks on our laps as a celebrated health writer leans on the podium and lifts a hand, saying, "What is food? Food is not entertainment or comfort or pleasure or love or distraction. Food is not good or evil. It's not your friend, it's not your mother, it's not your enemy." She scans the crowd, sighs at her notes. She seems to be disappointed in each and every one of us. "Food is nourishment, fuel, nutrient. Do not let yourselves become confused. It's time to get un-confused." She waves her diet book in the air. "Food is a *tool*. It can make you sick or keep you healthy, according to the choices you make — and those are entirely up to you."

Her talk is meant to be inspiring and uplifting. Afterward, though, after the rousing applause and the chatter, the screech of folding metal chairs pushed aside, the audience rushing out to snatch her book and spread the word, I'm feeling dispirited. On the drive home, I think about stopping at the market but can't imagine a thing to eat.

When I open the door, though I'd left only a few hours earlier, my daughter flies at my knees, crying, "MAMA!" as if I'd been away at sea. Every welcome-home is a moment of glory. I pick her up: She's solid in my arms, filled with surprising, sprightly strength. "What's for eat?" She holds my face with the palms of her hands, assuring that I'm looking directly at her.

It's weird to change houses soon after losing a parent — all shelter is gone, you feel turned out into the elements, a metaphysical homelessness. Oh, how I want to retreat into old comforts; I think of sweet ginger waffles, a bowl of butterscotch pudding. I nuzzle the warm crook below Gracie's right ear, and she chortles and shouts, "No!" Face in hands: Focus, woman. "For *eat?*"

Her gaze is pure and intent. It has the effect of an X on the map: You are here. I recognize this; the rest of life comes in such moments. The awareness that things are about to change. Gracie has an elemental and uncomplicated understanding of food, a sacred trust in her food-bringers. Like Bud moving between the table and the Qur'an, my grandmother going from church to oven — we tend to the body, but the spirit prevails. An old mote from Rumi comes back to me: "There are people moving back and forth across the door/ Don't go back to sleep."

Awaken or roll over, these are the choices. It's my turn, not only to make dinner but also to lead a child into the kitchen, to guide her through her appetites — both at and beyond the table. Bud had trouble sharing the kitchen, though he searched for and encouraged any traces of his culture in his children — through music and language and religion and temperament — he didn't like to give up that one power, as if it might compromise some essence of his spirit, his gift to us. But if you insist on always taking care of someone, it makes the moment when she must begin to take care of herself so much harder.

"I know a secret snack. Something the unicorns like to eat," I tell my daughter. Yes, she is interested.

On her step stool, Gracie watches me bring out the contents of the refrigerated drawers — a little romaine lettuce, some watermelon slices. Half a goat cheese. A cucumber. She wants to assist, messes be damned. Everything tastes better when you help to make it. We pluck some mint from the garden and check the tomato on the counter to see if it's gone mealy. She tears up the leaves, tosses the chopped pieces into a bowl, sprinkles on some pumpkin seeds we find in the back of the cupboard. In a jelly jar, I shake a deep-purple balsamic into olive oil, give it lots of salt and pepper, a bit of crushed garlic and honey and mustard, then drizzle it around. She samples some on a fingertip. We sit outside at the round iron table with two forks and Gracie eats only the cucumber and watermelon. I eat the rest of the salad with slow pleasure. We listen to the susurrus of the coconut and imperial palms, the fronds lowered, murmuring, full of secrets, like hair or fingers sweeping the air, speaking to us in forgotten languages.

You like what you like. Tastes are powerful, primal, intimate, uniquely your own. And the power to choose, to say, No, thank you, not this, is one of the most important powers — at the center of agency and pleasure. You are what you crave and fear and what you want. In a little while, I will snap a small, dark piece of chocolate in two: half for me and half for her. She tastes and hands it back: too bitter. Next week, I will pull out the jar of grape leaves, unscrew the tight lid, inhale their delicate brine, place a mixture of rice, lamb, and garlic at the center of each leaf's outspread "palm," and, slowly and with real care, begin rolling them up.

CHAPTER EIGHTEEN:
ART AND SUGAR

The trick, I'm told, is to see past the pleasure of the moment, which is transitory and deceptive. Sugar is a quick gratification, all about the instant. There is, I gather, a steadiness, a kind of sanity, to good nutrition.

What I CAN eat. It's a list, started on the advice of a nutritionist friend. The idea is, instead of staring at the things you shouldn't eat — chocolate, cookies, ice cream — think about all the good things you could. I keep it in the kitchen and, when I remember, add to it in a haphazard way: fruit salad, hummus, chicken soup, shish kabobs, Caprese salad, roast cauliflower. Everything but sugar goes on the list. Never-ending and never quite satisfying.

"You don't have to be quite *that* strict, do you?" my mother asks in a small voice. "No sweets at all?" She too inherited the sugar-fiend gene; she takes medication for her blood pressure.

"Well. . . ." My whole body feels like a sigh. "I don't know."

When I'm not baking, I dream of baking. I wake up with my jaw moving, chewing lovely invisible banana pancakes, edges caramelized and crisp, dripping with syrup. I try to distract myself. The main compartments of the refrigerator are crammed with lettuces and avocados and apples and berries and cucumbers and carrots. I own a yoga mat. I break down and buy big bricks of dark chocolate, store them in the freezer; it's a lot of work to carve off a few pieces, but every night I go after it with a butcher knife, trying to keep panic at bay.

Sugar and memory: I try to look at this squarely, tell myself that less of one doesn't have to mean less of the other. But memory runs out at the edges of the forest. And at the heart of my forest is a gingerbread house, enticing and mysterious and dark.

Sometimes I think the older you get, the more memories there are, and the deeper the forest becomes. A child thinks their life has one smooth shape — always moving straight ahead. Eventually, though, you start to see how crooked the path is, how the trees move closer, how birds have eaten your trail of bread crumbs. Even if you don't look, the past is right there, just behind your shoulder, and sometimes you lose track and can't tell what was a memory and what was a dream. You wake with the last notes of birdsong in your ears. Memories become sweeter and more persistent: Once again, I return to my childhood post at the stove after dinner, stirring and waiting for the scrim of foam to appear, pouring so carefully, taking Bud his *ahweh,* two teaspoons of sugar, barely stirred — don't break the foam. I recollect a night not long ago when I'd insisted Bud let me make the coffee, the way I did as a child. I said I would bring it to him.

I was stirring and waiting, and Gracie was leaning against her jiddo's leg, eating his cake. "It's okaaaay," Bud said, sneaking pieces for her with his fingers. "I don't mind. I never eat white food. Never. Nothing with sugar." He took another bite of cake, snuck another bite to Gracie. "She knows where to go — she knows go to Jiddo."

"Bud. Not the whole cake." I said this reflexively; he wouldn't listen.

His hand went to the top of his head, he had his apology-smile that wasn't an apology. "I can't help it." This is what he said when Gracie demanded a toy or to be carried, or she hid behind him from a scolding, or ate everything on his plate. He ran his hand over her head. "We know each other." Bud repeated the story again, how his own father knocked on his head and said, What's in there? You got rocks for your brains? One of the cold memories we tried to protest and protect him from. But he didn't mind; he suspected, in his deepest self, that he was still a demanding wild child. That he connected with our three-year-old better than almost any adult could.

"Look at this one! My baby. How did you do this, Ya Bah?" He touched his face. "My grandbaby — same curly head, same big eye, same curly nose. How did you bring me this baby? It's an *us'meh*." His eyes were dark. "She's an *us'meh,* from Allah, straight to me. Right out of the sky."

I stared at the black round of coffee, stirring.

"You know who you named after?" he asked her.

"No!" She tipped her head sideways, sagged, hung on his knees. She knew.

"Your sitto Grace. She tried to feed me. Your grandma right here, she takes me home to meet her mom. You should see what your sitto tries to feed me. . . ."

337

Not this story again.

"What?" Gracie cried. "What Sitto feed you?"

"Oh, I've told you this one before, I know I have!" Bud said, waiting to be begged before he began. "First, on the table — these shrimps, I never seen anything like. Huge like *soursour.* . . ." Cockroaches.

Oh, that wonderful old memory! Bud shook his head. His half-frowning, sorrowful smile. "I miss her. She was a good fighter. Grace loved to fight. To this day I miss her."

The cravings go away, people tell me. I slather apple slices with peanut butter, construct the biggest fruit salads in the world. At my desk, I open books about health and wellness, then all at once I'm on the floor in the dining room, rereading sections of Edith Wharton; I don't remember how I got there. I try to rehabilitate myself. Most of the nutrition books have helpful mottoes about moderation and inspiration and can-do. Each day, I try to learn the tiniest lessons, and then right away I forget them. I may be beyond hope.

Testing or torturing myself, I offer to make salted chocolate brownies for Gracie's preschool class. When they're done baking and cut into squares, I offer her a few test pieces. She eats two and leaves the last one. "Didn't you like them?" I ask.

"I loved them," she says, surprised.

"But?" I hold up the last piece.

She shrugs. "I'm done."

She is, I realize, the most uncomplicated eater I've ever met, her appetite squared neatly, ingeniously with her body. There is something here for me to pay attention to: learn to answer the body, not the mind.

I come up with my own mantra to tape to the fridge: Bake your own dessert. Don't eat the whole thing.

"You learn food by feel, not on a paper." Aunt Aya's smile was strong and bright, though her lipstick bled into a million cracks around her mouth. In her seventies, my aunt still wore the same makeup. "Why would you write down how to cook?"

"You mean. . . ." I hesitated, forty years old, beginning my third marriage, yet around her, eternally seven. I'd just made the mistake of requesting one of her "recipes." "What *do* you mean?"

She shook her head and settled back against her divan, arms folded. "It's like learning to speak French. You don't do it in a *classroom.* You do it running around

Montmartre, calling for cabs, drinking Pernod."

I frowned, considering this analogy, and she stood and seized my wrist, narrow fingers digging into the bone. "Come on, then. Come, come, come. I'll show you everything."

It was late in the day and the long shadows made her stone-floored kitchen cool and dim. She hustled around, requiring an enormous, flat tray that her sixty-nine-year-old housekeeper, Mrs. Mahmoudy, had just finished drying. There was a bit of a tug of war, which my aunt won, waving Mrs. Mahmoudy out of the room with one hand.

"Now this — this is a true Palestinian dish," she said. "Your grandmother Aniseh — her knafeh? The Arabs have an expression: You're so beautiful you make me go insane. That was her knafeh. Like a vision. The Palestinians love it because knafeh is like a home — which is something everyone longs for."

Aya sat in a carved wooden chair and gave directions while I scurried, stirring and chopping. Occasionally she would break in to show me the correct manner of mixing together the semolina and the flour, then she'd go back to her chair. Unlike my grandmother, who'd loved the actual bak-

340

ing, for Aya baking was an excuse to hold forth. "Some people, I'm told, find it acceptable to color the butter with some sort of dye." She touched thumb and forefinger to her forehead, as if the very thought of this brought on physical pain.

"No dye," I echoed.

"Saffron only. There's no point to being pretty without poetry."

We brushed the tray with a poetic saffron-yellow clarified butter then covered this with toasted shredded dough. "The story of knafeh is that the base is like a nest — these shreds are like the twigs. And the nest holds — what do you think it holds?"

"An egg?"

She gave me a long, pleased *no:* "It holds a marriage." Aya brought the tips of her fingers together.

She pointed out sparse places on the tray; I leaned over and tufted it with more dough. She produced a bowl filled with tiny cheese curds, which were then scattered over the dough. "The cheese is mild — like the heart of a good husband. Next comes the syrup, sweet as a bride. Not too much! Nothing worse than too sweet." She monitored as I poured a thin stream of attar over the pastry. "Nobody expects cheese and sweet to get along, but you arrange their marriage, and see? They are crazy in love."

It was well past midnight and a slim silver moon hung in the windows when the knafeh was pulled from the oven. Aunt Aya placed two plates on the table and used a flat spatula to cut large helpings of the pastry. I apologized to my aunt for keeping her up so late. Half an hour earlier, Mrs. Mahmoudy had come into the kitchen to ask rather pointedly who we thought was going to clean up. She departed without waiting for an answer. "Oh, this isn't late," my aunt scoffed. "Things are just starting. In a few hours, the man in the tower will be calling for prayers. Knafeh is for breakfast time."

I closed my eyes, drifting on the buttery scent. Back in the States, when I've made knafeh for friends, they sometimes don't like it, uncertain about the mixture of melting cheese and crisp, sweet dough, a dish in between dinner and dessert. "Gram should've tried this," I said, half to myself. "I don't know. Maybe not."

Aya smiled thinly. She'd visited America several times, yet she seemed always to be humoring me when I mentioned aspects of my life at home — as if it were all my little fantasy. Then her eyes lit up and she clapped her hands. "Oh! The one named Grace? Who made the Catholic cookies?"

I'd forgotten. Twenty-five years ago, Grace had tasted some baklava that Aya had made during a visit to see Bud and his family, The Americans. As soon as she returned to New Jersey, my grandmother swathed a tin of Wurstcakes in tissue paper and bubble wrap and mailed it overseas to my aunt. A few months after that, I opened Gram's cupboard to find rows of little cellophane bags filled with brightly colored, unlabeled spices, her whole pantry smelling of Jordan. "Where did these come from?" I asked, agape. I picked up a bag and sniffed something I was pretty sure was zataar.

"I have my sources," Grace said smugly.

In this far-off kitchen, ten years after Grace's death, it seemed as though she might stroll back in at any moment. Memory persists in present tense, immortal. I felt the closeness of things, the moon shining on Jordan and New Jersey. I felt how time collapses and things draw together in unexpected ways. Grace and Aya never met each other, yet they recognized each other, their solitary, unconventional lives. In a few months' time, I would begin the process of contemplating parenthood. If there was a way to inscribe such things, I would have asked Aya for her advice, to describe the steps she'd taken toward attaining courage

— learning how to know what you want, learning how to be brave enough to pursue it. But, by that point, I was already beginning to suspect you couldn't write it down: You had to do it by feel.

"Your grandmother Grace," Aunt Aya said, "would have loved the knafeh."

The advice-givers are the ones who can make you afraid, but they're also the ones who offer courage. Both things. They do it by showing you the ways they grew stronger and the things that gave them joy. The art is in what you choose to pay attention to.

Scowling, Mrs. Mahmoudy came back into the kitchen, plump hands propped on her hips. "I'm not cleaning this." She groaned herself into a chair and looked at the knafeh as if it had just insulted her. "Where is the coffee? You don't expect normal people to eat this without coffee?"

I started to get up, but my aunt was already at the stove. At one a.m., there were thimbles of black coffee and three plates of knafeh. We were on some different sort of clock where stars and planets swam past the windows; inside, we were impervious to all but the pastry. It was lustrous and supple, its ingredients held in equipoise. If deliciousness is a kind of grace, this was it. Beside my aunt, at her kitchen table, I ate knafeh and drank in moonlight, and, brave or not, I knew I was about to begin something.

I told my aunt's story about the mild husband and sweet wife to Mrs. Mahmoudy, who appeared bewildered by it. Then, sitting straight, she waved a bite of knafeh on the fork and asked my aunt, "You said the mild and the sweet, but who is the crunchy, Aya? Where does the crisp dough fit into that perfect marriage?"

Aya didn't turn. Mrs. Mahmoudy had been her housekeeper for sixty years, and they no longer needed to look at each other. She sipped her coffee, took a bite, and said, with a trace of a smile, "The crunch is the mother-in-law."

When you're a bit innocent of the world, many things are unexpected. What's supposed to keep you safe is what makes you afraid. The thing you can't have is the thing you want the most. It takes forever just to get to the beginning. No matter how many times I write down the instructions, I forget it all, just as faithfully, and need to study it again. Art and pastry and memory and risk: The days arrange themselves into stories, which are themselves just moments, mere moments.

A moment to look up, to the window above the desk. I see my husband and my daughter outside on the lawn.

Throw out the sugar, turn the art toward the walls, switch off the screens.

Scott swings Grace up onto his shoulders and they're off to explore. She lifts her fingers and strums the palm fronds, the neighbor's dogs bound at their heels; my daughter calls to them, wanting them to jump higher, knowing they'll never reach her there, up on such high shoulders. I watch them go. Someone should see about dinner. I should get back to my writing. But I want to run after them.

I think I will.

ACKNOWLEDGMENTS

I'd especially like to thank:

Andrea Gollin; Joy Harris; Alane Salierno Mason; Marie Pantojan; Lorraine Mercer; Hagop Kantarjian; Carey McKearnan; Adrienne and Frank Curson; Thomas Wolf; Whitney Otto and John Riley.

for listening, reading, holding my hand, and not letting me off the hook,

And my family:

for living it with me

and Scott:

for making it possible.

Check Out Receipt

Upper Merion Township Library
610-265-4805
www.mclinc.org/umtl

Tuesday, July 19, 2016 10:17:55 AM

Title: Life without a recipe [text (large print)
] : a memoir
Due: 08/09/2016

Total items: 1

Thank You!

ABOUT THE AUTHOR

Diana Abu-Jaber is the award-winning author of four novels, including *Crescent*, and a previous memoir, *The Language of Baklava*. She and her family divide time between Miami, Florida, and Portland, Oregon.

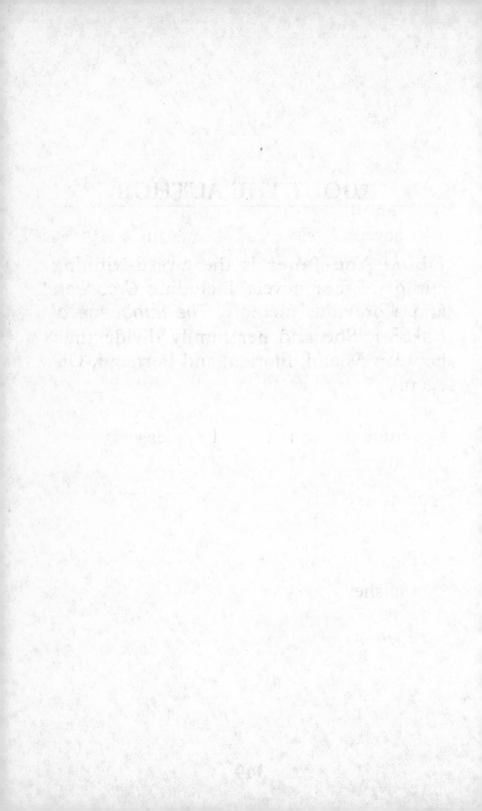

The employees of Thorndike Press hope you have enjoyed this Large Print book. All our Thorndike, Wheeler, and Kennebec Large Print titles are designed for easy reading, and all our books are made to last. Other Thorndike Press Large Print books are available at your library, through selected bookstores, or directly from us.

For information about titles, please call:
(800) 223-1244

or visit our Web site at:
http://gale.cengage.com/thorndike

To share your comments, please write:
Publisher
Thorndike Press
10 Water St., Suite 310
Waterville, ME 04901